Moral
Leadership

Thomas J. Sergiovanni

Moral
Leadership

GETTING TO
THE HEART
OF SCHOOL
IMPROVEMENT

 Jossey-Bass Publishers · San Francisco

Credits are on page 173.

For sales outside the United States contact Maxwell/Macmillan International Publishing Group, 866 Third Avenue, New York, New York 10022

Printed on acid-free paper and manufactured in the United States of America

---

Library of Congress Cataloging-in-Publication Data

Sergiovanni, Thomas J.
    Moral leadership: getting to the heart of school improvement / Thomas J. Sergiovanni.
       p. cm. — (The Jossey-Bass education series)
    Includes bibliographical references and index.
    ISBN 1-55542-400-7
    1. School management and organization — United States.
  2. Leadership. 3. Ethics — United States. I. Title. II. Series.
LB2805.S524 1992
371.2'00973 — dc20   91-31187
                                      CIP

FIRST EDITION
HB Printing   10 9 8 7 6 5 4 3 2 1   *Code 9205*

The Jossey-Bass
Education Series

Contents

Preface

Leadership is not a magic solution for improving schools. Moreover, focusing on leadership separately from such issues as school governance, finance, parental involvement, curriculum reform, labor relations, diversity, teaching and learning, and assessment may cover up problems and provide symptomatic relief that makes us feel good but changes little that matters. Unfortunately, there is no primrose path to school improvement.

Still, leadership is important, and the kind and quality of leadership we have will help determine, for better or for worse, the kinds of schools we have. One theme of this book is that the type of leadership now being emphasized may be getting in the way of school improvement. Instead of more of this type of leadership, we may actually need less.

Calling for less leadership needs some explaining, for it is commonly accepted that strong, forceful, direct leadership from principals and other administrators is important in creating effective schools. This sentiment is sometimes summed up by prescriptions for principals to become the instructional leaders of their schools. The evidence offered in support of this position is that when schools are in trouble, strong and direct instructional leadership from principals helps them get better. The question that is not asked is: what kind of leadership do schools need once they are out of trouble? Further, what should our stance be if strong instructional leadership from the principal continues to be needed for improvement after two or three years of effort? For example, say that teachers, after several years, still need someone to give them direction, monitor them, provide them with inservice training, evaluate them, and reward and punish them, so that the job of teaching will be done properly. Does that mean the principal has failed as a leader?

I believe that one of the reasons why improving schools is so difficult is that we give too much attention to direct leadership. Instead of focusing almost exclusively on leadership as something forceful, direct, and interpersonal, we can get a better handle on improving schools over the long term by giving at least equal attention to providing substitutes for leadership. Substitutes for leadership can make leadership itself less necessary.

Improving schools involves identifying the right leverage points for change. Current conceptions of leadership, however, steer us toward school-improvement strategies that often miscalculate which leverage points are high and which are low. A high leverage point leads to significant, long-lasting improvements, with a minimum of effort; a low leverage point, by contrast, requires a lot of effort but produces meager results. Peter M. Senge (1990a) suggests that in applying improvement leverage, the best results tend to come from smaller, more focused efforts, rather than from large-scale efforts. Moreover, the points that have the highest leverage are often the least obvious ones.

In schools, low-leverage improvement strategies typically involve large-scale changes in how schools are structured and operated (that is, new forms of school governance, massive curriculum projects, complex evaluation systems, ambitious training programs for teachers, and new designs for organizing schooling). Too often, the results are disappointing. Part of the problem is the difficulty of getting these initiatives started and, once they are started, of sustaining them. In addition, a very direct, intense, draining style of interpersonal leadership is often needed to keep initiatives going, to motivate people, and to monitor performance and make sure that things are going the way they should. For the most part, low-leverage improvement strategies tend to change the way things look but not the way they work.

If Senge (1990a) is correct, far more attention will have to be given to more subtle, less obvious, and higher leverage points in efforts to improve schools. Two such points, proposed in this book, are to expand the value structure underlying the way in which leadership is understood and practiced and to expand the bases of authority for the practice of leadership.

The management values now considered legitimate are biased toward rationality, logic, objectivity, the importance of self-interest, explicitness, individuality, and detachment. *Emphasizing* these values causes us to *neglect* emotions, the importance of group membership, sense and meaning, morality, self-sacrifice, duty, and obligation as *additional* values. Furthermore, the bases of authority for today's leadership practice rely heavily on bureaucracy, psychological knowledge or skill, and the technical rationality that emerges from theory and research. *Emphasizing* these three bases causes us to *neglect* professional and moral authority as *additional* bases for leadership practice.

The words *emphasizing, neglect,* and *additional* are italicized in the preceding paragraph because they are important in understanding the position taken in this book. I argue, for example, that full, rich leadership practice cannot be developed if one set of values or one basis of authority is simply substituted for another. What we need is an expanded theoretical and operational foundation for leadership practice that will give balance to the full range of values and bases of authority. I refer to this expanded foundation as the *moral dimension in leadership*.

Giving attention to the moral dimension may require us to reinvent the concept of leadership itself. For this to happen, many common, taken-for-granted notions about leadership will have to be challenged and changed. What now seems obvious may well turn out to be less important, and what now seems less obvious may well turn out to be more important.

For example, it seems obvious that leadership breeds followership. Less obvious is the idea that the practice of followership provides the basis for leadership.

It seems obvious that leadership should be explicit. Less obvious is the idea that substitutes for leadership may make explicit leadership less necessary.

It seems obvious that schools are organizations. Less obvious is the idea that transforming schools from organizations to communities may be a key to school improvement.

It seems obvious that teachers and schools need to be empowered. Less obvious is the idea that empowerment may have more to do with obligations and commitments than with discretion.

It seems obvious that collegiality involves providing the conditions and arrangements that enable teachers and others to work together. Less obvious is the idea that collegiality is also a form of professional virtue that comes from within.

It seems obvious that people are motivated by self-interest. Less obvious is the idea that emotions and social bonds may be more important sources of motivation.

It seems obvious that leadership is a form of behavior. Less obvious is the idea that leadership is also a form of stewardship.

Overview of the Contents

In this book, I seek to build a theory of school leadership practice based on moral authority, but to establish such practice requires the value structure of and authority basis for school leadership to be expanded.

Chapter One critiques traditional views of leadership and discusses the reasons why they have not worked well in the past. An argument is then made for reinventing leadership in a way that joins process and substance and accounts not only for the hand of leadership but also for its head and its heart. One key to this effort is to expand the values thought to be legitimate in school management. I argue, for example, that sense experience, intuition, sacred authority, and emotion must be considered to be as legitimate as secular authority, science, and deductive logic, the three values that now dominate management thought.

In Chapter Two, I examine what motivates and inspires teachers and principals to work in extraordinary ways. In the past, these questions have been answered in ways that seriously underestimated the nature of human potential. I point out that emotions, values, and our connections with other people count a great deal but are seriously underplayed as sources of motivation. Further, the exclusive use of material incentives and psychological rewards as the basis for motivational strategies assumes that all that matters is self-interest. But the evidence is overwhelming that teachers and principals regularly sacrifice self-interest for other ideas and ideals. I discuss the consequences of neglecting the full range of human potential and offer a perspective on motivation based on moral authority.

The sources of authority for leadership are important. Different sources have different consequences. Chapter Three discusses the sources, pointing out that we now rely almost exclusively on bureaucratic authority, psychological authority, and technical-rational authority. For example, we ask teachers to comply because of bureaucratic requirements, or in response to the leader's personality and interpersonal skills, or because of what the research says. Important as these sources may be, they are not as powerful as moral authority as a basis for school leadership practice.

Chapter Four discusses substitutes for leadership, maintaining that the more we are able to integrate substitute models into the school, the more likely it is that teachers and others will become self-managed, and the less important leadership itself will become. The two substitutes discussed in Chapter Four are the norms that emerge (1) when schools are transformed from organizations to communities and (2) when professionalism is viewed not only as a statement of competence but also as a virtue.

Chapter Five examines still another important substitute for leadership: the potential for satisfaction that can come from the work of the school itself.

In Chapter Six, I discuss the difference between a leadership practice that casts teachers in a subordinate role and one that helps them become followers. The links between building followership and fostering self-management are explored, and suggestions are made for developing followership.

In Chapter Seven, I discuss the importance of collegiality

in building a morally responsive school community. Collegiality is often believed to have something to do with warm interpersonal relationships, on the one hand, and with school arrangements that force teachers to work together, on the other. In its best form, however, collegiality comes from within as teachers feel the necessity of and the responsibility for sharing and working together. Expressed in this way, collegiality can be understood as a form of professional virtue.

Chapter Eight, in a discussion of the virtuous school, reprises the themes of expanding management values and sources of authority for leadership, tapping higher levels of human potential, providing substitutes for leadership, building followership, and understanding collegiality as a professional virtue. I give attention to the importance of building a covenant of shared values and show how covenants work in practice. I then offer suggestions for deciding what should be included in a school covenant. Characteristics of the virtuous school, as I envision them, are listed, and readers are invited to reflect on their own ideas.

In Chapter Nine, I say that, with morally responsive leadership, principals and teachers will become stewards and servants. There remains a place for command leadership, instructional leadership, and interpersonal leadership, but the heart of one's leadership practice is to become the embodiment of one's ministerial role. Building a covenant of shared values; empowerment concerned with duties and obligations, as well as with discretion; collegiality, understood as a form of professional virtue; leadership by outrage; kindling outrage in others — these are principles of leadership proposed in the chapter, and examples are given of their use in school practice.

Expanding the value structure of and authority bases for leadership in the manner suggested in this book can bring to leadership practice a set of powerful ideas for influencing what and how people think and feel. This is strong medicine; but the medicine now thought to be the cure for our leadership problems may become toxic if it is misapplied, and can make matters even worse. I try to deal with this difficult issue in the epilogue. I considered making it the prologue to this book, to set the tone;

but because the tone is so negative, I reconsidered and decided to hide it at the end. The dilemma—to forewarn, or to hide?—can be resolved if the epilogue is read first.

For Whom This Book Is Intended

This book is addressed to principals, supervisors, superintendents, and other school administrators who face moral dilemmas every day. My intent was to write a short book, to provoke and raise consciousness without being too pedantic or intrusive, and I hope that I have succeeded. This book can also serve as a counterpoint to the various textbooks, commonly used in university courses, on principalship, leadership, and organizational behavior. School board members, lay and professional policymakers, and parents may also find the book useful in helping them rethink what school leadership is and can become.

Acknowledgments

My views on leadership owe much to the writings of Warren Bennis and Amitai Etzioni. Bennis has always seemed to sense the importance of leadership's sacred dimensions. Etzioni has long reminded us of the importance of norms and membership connections as we make sense of our lives. Their work continues to exert influence; indeed, much of today's literature on culture and on moral authority in leadership rests on the shoulders of these two giants.

Anecdotes and stories not formally listed in the references were contributed by principals, superintendents, and others, as part of my ongoing research on how school leaders think and on the practical theories they use to guide their practice. Given the number of participants, I am not able to acknowledge individually all the people who helped me, but I am deeply grateful for their generosity and for all that they have taught me about leadership.

San Antonio, Texas   Thomas J. Sergiovanni
December 1991

◈ The Author

THOMAS J. SERGIOVANNI is Lillian Radford Professor of Education at Trinity University, San Antonio, Texas. He received his B.S. degree (1958) from the State University of New York, Geneseo, his M.A. degree (1959) from Teachers College, Columbia University, and his Ed.D. degree (1966) from the University of Rochester.

From 1958 to 1964, he was an elementary school teacher and science consultant in New York state and taught in the teacher education program at the State University of New York, Buffalo. In 1966, he began nineteen years of service on the faculty of educational administration at the University of Illinois, Urbana–Champaign, and chaired the department for seven years.

At Trinity University, Sergiovanni teaches in the school leadership program and in the five-year teacher education program. He is senior fellow at the Center for Educational Leadership and director of the Trinity Principals' Center. A former associate editor of *Educational Administration Quarterly*, he serves on the editorial boards of the *Journal of Educational Research*, the *Journal of Curriculum and Supervision*, the *Journal of Personnel Evaluation in Education*, and *Teaching Education*. He has broad interests in school leadership and the supervision and evaluation of teaching. Among his recent books are *Schooling for Tomorrow: Directing Reforms to Issues that Count* (1989, with John Moore), *Value-Added Leadership: How to Get Extraordinary Performance in Schools* (1990), and *The Principalship: A Reflective Practice Perspective* (1991, second edition).

Moral
Leadership

1

Reinventing Leadership

Asked to share her views on leadership, Diana Lam (1990), then superintendent of the Chelsea, Massachusetts, schools, wrote, "I believe leadership is an attitude which informs behavior rather than a set of discrete skills or qualities, whether innate or acquired" (p.1). To her, the key qualities needed in school leadership are an understanding of how children and adults learn and keep on learning and the ability to build communities of learners: "Leadership belongs to everyone. . . . Our role is to cultivate the leadership potential of every single employee, student, and parent in our school system" (p. 2). Why is the distinction between leadership attitude and leadership skill important? "Our vision informs our work," and "we are the leaders and our views shape the views of others" (p. 3). What kind of leaders do we need? "We need leaders who understand how children and adults learn—and keep on learning. . . who understand how to build communities of learners. Yes, we need leaders with skills—but skills can be learned. I do not know how to change someone's heart" (p. 1).

This kind of talk—about attitudes and values informing our leadership practice; about how visions, for better or for worse, frame our views and the views of others; about leadership's belonging to everyone; about the placement of content and substance (teaching and learning, building learning communities) over process and skills—is a new kind of leadership talk. It represents the voice of practice, a voice largely neglected in the traditional school-leadership literature.

The Failure of Leadership

The topic of leadership represents one of social science's greatest disappointments. After fifty years of steady work, social science can tell us very little about the subject. In 1959, for example, the noted leadership theorist Warren Bennis wrote, "Of all the hazy and confounding areas in social psychology, leadership theory undoubtedly contends for top nomination. Probably more has been written and less is known about leadership than any other topic in the behavioral sciences" (p. 259). Fifteen years later, Ralph Stogdill (1974) wrote, "Four decades of research on leadership has produced a bewildering mass of findings. . . . It is difficult to know what, if anything, has been convincingly demonstrated by replicative research. The endless accumulation of empirical data has not produced an integrated understanding of leadership" (p. viii). More recently, in their best-selling book on leadership, Bennis and Burt Nanus (1985) wrote, "Literally thousands of empirical investigations of leaders have been conducted in the last seventy-five years alone, but no clear and unequivocal understanding exists as to what distinguishes leaders from nonleaders and, perhaps more important, what distinguishes *effective* leaders from *ineffective* leaders and *effective* organizations from *ineffective* organizations." Pointing out that "never have so many labored so long to say so little" (p. 4), these authors confess to having lost faith in traditional conceptions of leadership.

For the most part, the study of leadership has dwelt on issues of style and levels of decision making, assessing the consequences of their variations for followers' satisfaction, individual compliance and performance, and organizational effectiveness. Which style is better—warm or cold, autocratic or democratic, task or relationship, directive or participatory, initiating structure or consideration, production emphasis or personal emphasis? When is it best to "tell, sell, participate and delegate" (Hersey and Blanchard, 1988)? Do circumstances of the job favor the "related, dedicated, separated, or integrated" leadership style (Reddin, 1970)? *Best* is defined as what gets subordinates to do what the leader wants and be happy about it. If enough subordinates respond appropriately, then the organization presumably will be more effective. When this research on leadership is packaged for popular consumption, *leadership* becomes little more than a buzzword — patter for workshop providers and an elixir for policymakers intent on improving schools. Both promise much but deliver little.

Why has the yield in practice been so dismal, given all our efforts? I believe there are two reasons for the failure of leadership. First, we have come to view leadership as behavior rather than action, as something psychological rather than spiritual, as having to do with persons rather than ideas. Second, in trying to understand what drives leadership, we have overemphasized bureaucratic, psychological, and technical-rational authority, seriously neglecting professional and moral authority. In the first instance, we have separated the hand of leadership from its head and its heart. In the second, we have separated the process of leadership from its substance. The result has been a leadership literature that borders on vacuity and a leadership practice that is not leadership at all. These are harsh words, not offered lightly.

The bright side of the picture is that in our schools, corporations, and other institutions, a practice is emerging that requires us to redefine the concept of leadership. The field is ahead of the theory. As a result, our literature and our official conversation about leadership do not take enough account of successful practice.

This book is an effort to catch up. The crux of my argument is that if we want our theory to reflect emerging practice, then we need to move the moral dimension in leadership away from the periphery and right to the center of inquiry, discussion, and practice.

The Managerial Mystique

Abraham Zaleznik (1989) of the Harvard Business School sees the failure of leadership as a result of the managerial mystique. This mystique represents the dominant "world view" of management theory and practice and is reflected in the curricula of

most university preparation programs, in the mainstream literature of the field, in the rules and regulations of the governing
bodies that certify administrators, and in the management-
appraisal systems of our schools and other institutions. This
world view has emerged over the course of the twentieth century
as management has become professionalized (Tyack and
Hansot, 1982) and is now accepted as the image of what good
management is and how leadership is best expressed. According
to Zaleznik (1989; p. 2), "As it evolved in practice, the mystique
required managers to dedicate themselves to process, structures, roles, and indirect forms of communication and to ignore
ideas, people, emotions, and direct talk. It deflected attention
from the realities of business [and schools], while it reassured
and rewarded those who believed in the mystique."

In practice, the managerial mystique represents a tacit
compact among too many policymakers, administrators, and
academics, which places process before substance and form
before function. So strongly does the mystique adhere to belief
in the right methods that the methods themselves become surrogates for results. It also holds so firmly to the belief in management controls, as the way to overcome human shortcomings
and enhance productivity, that the controls become ends in
themselves.

The result is an emphasis on doing things right, at the
expense of doing the right things. In schools, improvement
plans become substitutes for improvement outcomes. Scores on
teacher-appraisal systems become substitutes for good teaching.
Accumulation of credits in courses and inservice workshops
becomes a substitute for changes in practice. Discipline plans
become substitutes for student control. Leadership styles become substitutes for purpose and substance. Congeniality becomes a substitute for collegiality. Cooperation becomes a substitute for commitment. Compliance becomes a substitute for
results. Where the managerial mystique rules, school administrators are forced to do rather than decide, to implement rather
than lead. Too often, the results are "trained incapacity" (Veblen,
1973) and "goal displacement" (Merton, 1968).

Consider trained incapacity. When policies and practices

are based on the managerial mystique, there is a tendency to focus knowledge, attention, and skills so narrowly that principals and teachers become incapable of thinking and acting beyond their prescribed roles. Management expert Tom Peters describes an example of trained incapacity. A McKinsey and Company study of U.S. engineering practices revealed that engineers in the United States develop concepts and pass them along to designers, who then transform the concepts into designs. Draftspersons put the designs on paper. Finally, checkers follow up the drawing details. In Japan, by contrast, engineers perform a broader array of tasks. McKinsey researcher Leif Soderberg explains, "A U.S. destroyer requiring a major hull repair pulled into a Japanese shipyard. A [Japanese] repair team of engineers, supervisors, and shipworkers swarmed all over the damaged ship. Drawings were prepared twenty yards away from the hull while damaged sections were removed. No review or signature by higher levels in the engineering department, no bids processed by purchasing—just a team totally dedicated to the ship" (Peters, 1990, p. 11B). The ship's captain was convinced that the three-day repair in Japan would have taken sixty days in the United States. We could easily relate a dozen or so similar stories from our own experience in schools.

Now consider goal displacement, which is shown in the tendency for schools to lose sight of their purposes, allowing instrumental processes and procedures to become ends in themselves. Rules are enforced because they exist; the motions of classroom supervision and evaluation are repeated in thousands of classrooms every day, with little effect. School-based management becomes an end, rather than a means of restructuring. School-improvement plans are considered to be the same thing as school improvement.

Trained incapacity and goal displacement comprise powerful scripts that program what we do. The result is a gridlock on the kind of thinking and initiative needed to resolve problems, as well as on the leadership drive and vision necessary to inspire extraordinary commitment and performance. This gridlock represents a conspiracy of mediocrity. To break the gridlock, leadership behavior must once again be joined with substance, and management processes must once again be joined with purposes.

The Head, Heart, and Hand of Leadership

What is leadership, anyway? For example, is Steve Johnson, the principal of Mark Twain Middle School, San Antonio, Texas, a leader? Ana Garcia (1988, p. 4) describes him at work as follows:

> Being a principal for him is not just a role but a function. He does anything and everything that needs to be done to make Twain a more successful place. He can even be seen cleaning tables off in the cafeteria, if needed. This is a great model for others. Being a principal for Steve Johnson is definitely a vocation. It is his life, not just part of his life. His family is also very involved with this process Twain is going through. Many days, his wife can be seen at Twain typing and editing reports or important documents for the school. They can both be seen at the various extracurricular or curriculum-related activities during the week. They attend all the athletic events, school programs, and even special events, such as the enactment of the Battle of the Alamo at dawn. Johnson is not a "tidy" administrator but a practical one. He always attempts to emphasize sense and meaning. Things that are done in a school should be done because they have a purpose, not because they have always been done a particular way. Purpose is built into Twain's everyday life. As the school counselor explained, "Things just seem less out of control with Mr. Johnson here. Also, things are communicated more openly. We are given an explanation for why things are done. There is not a mystery behind policy, and if things are not being done effectively, we attempt to find a better way. Business as usual is not promoted. Things make more sense, and our philoso-

phy is so much more positive than it was even last year." To Steve Johnson, leadership is not a right but a responsibility. He is always looking after the best interests of the school.

If one accepts the definitions of leadership that have dominated the literature over the past half-century, then Steve Johnson is not a leader. Why? Because most discussions of leadership focus on such issues as the leader's interpersonal style or behavior, or on the leader's ability to match his or her style to the needs of subordinates.

Unquestionably, there is value in charting and understanding what we can call the *hand of leadership*; some behaviors do seem to make more sense, in certain circumstances, than others do. But the hand alone is not powerful enough to account for what leadership is; indeed, it may not represent leadership at all. If we want to understand what Steve Johnson is all about, or if we want to understand any other leader's behavior, we have to examine the *heart* and the *head* of leadership, too.

The heart of leadership has to do with what a person believes, values, dreams about, and is committed to—the person's *personal vision*, to use the popular term. But it is more than vision. It is the person's interior world, which becomes the foundation of her or his reality.

The head of leadership has to do with the mindscapes, or theories of practice, that leaders develop over time, and with their ability, in light of these theories, to reflect on the situations they face. Reflection, combined with personal vision and an internal system of values, becomes the basis of leadership strategies and actions. If the heart and the head are separated from the hand, then the leader's actions, decisions, and behaviors cannot be understood.

The head of leadership is shaped by the heart and drives the hand; in turn, reflections on decisions and actions affirm or reshape the heart and the head. This interaction can be depicted as follows:

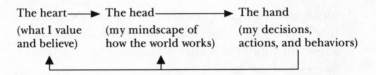

The heart ──▶ The head ──────────▶ The hand

(what I value   (my mindscape of   (my decisions,
and believe)   how the world works)   actions, and behaviors)

The connections and interactions shown in this diagram mean that becoming a successful leader requires recapturing the head from the managerial mystique—in other words, changing our mindscapes, which is not easy. For example, we may have to reject much of our management training. We may also have to view much of the existing management literature and its prescriptions for leadership practice as more historical than functional—as descriptions of yesterday's state of the art, but not today's.

Mindscapes—the mental pictures in our heads about how the world works—are often tacitly held. They program what we believe counts, help create our realities, and provide a basis for decisions. What we do makes sense if it matches our mindscapes. And different mindscapes represent different realities: what makes sense with one mindscape may not make sense with another. Different realities can lead people to behave quite differently.

Likewise, different mindscapes lead school administrators to interpret the same events differently. For example, Martin Maehr and his associates at the National Center for Research on School Leadership, at the University of Illinois, Urbana, equipped fifty principals in the greater Chicago area with beepers, asking them to record what they were doing when randomly paged (all fifty were paged at the same time). One day, the beepers went off at 3:15 P.M., when most of the principals were dealing with the school buses. One principal recorded the event this way: "supervising school bus loading." Another recorded the same event this way: "working with kids to encourage and raise expectations of success as they board the buses" (Sashkin, 1990, p. 16).

Mindscapes raise the question of whether an objective world really exists. Rorty (cited in Benjamin, 1990) says yes: for the most part, the world does exist independently of our beliefs, but the *truth* about the world does not; truth for each of us is a function of how we see and describe the world—in other words, of our mindscapes.

Not all management and leadership mindscapes are equal. Some fit the world of practice better than others. The better the fit, the more successful the practice will be. One of the themes of this book is that traditional mindscapes do not fit today's world of practice very well and are unresponsive to what people want from their jobs. On the one hand, traditional mindscapes do not take the nonlinear, loosely connected, messy context of managerial work into account; on the other, they underestimate the potential of principals, parents, and teachers to respond for reasons other than self-interest. In both cases, the need is for a leadership practice that can compel people to respond from within.

A Question of Values

Values play an important part in constructing an administrator's mindscape and in determining leadership practice. Steve Johnson clears tables in the cafeteria for a very good reason—the same reason why another principal might not clear tables. The second principal might spend her or his time and energy expressing a strategy of "expect and inspect": have expectations for what you want from teachers, communicate those expectations clearly, and establish a system of monitoring, to be sure that teachers are complying according to the script. "Expect and inspect" is a strategy that Steve Johnson rarely thinks about: he does not like to think of himself as a leader. In his words, "This is a good school. There are wonderful things going on here, and I don't think I did anything to cause them to happen. I just want people to be able to teach" (Garcia, 1988).

Mark Twain teacher Pat Clayworth remarks, "Steve Johnson is a good principal. He's not interested in his professional career. Everything he does revolves around what is best for the classrooms, students, and teachers" (Garcia, 1988, p. 4). Johnson understands how to communicate what is important and uses himself as a model. He would reject the notion that a principal

should be a "strong instructional leader." He would be more
comfortable with the notion of "servant leadership." (We will
examine the mystery and power of servant leadership in greater
detail in the last chapter of this book.)

Why does Johnson view his job differently from the way
the "expect and inspect" principal does? It is partly because what
each principal chooses to do is a function of the heart and the
head, and the substance of these is a question of values. Values
may not get much play in curricula of management and leadership in universities or in staff development academies, but
they count in practice. To some superintendents, for example,
successfully implementing a complicated mandate from the
board of education is enough of an indicator of a "fair day's
work"; to Rene Townsend, superintendent of the Vista, California, Unified School District, it is not.

Townsend was given a mandate from her school board to
change eleven elementary schools and three middle schools
from a traditional to a year-round calendar. Because of enroll-
ment pressures, the job had to be done within a year and a half.
Working carefully and tirelessly with her cabinet, Townsend
appointed several advisory committees, conducted successful
negotiations with the teachers' association, and set up a work-
able plan. She personally launched an exhausting campaign to
keep all concerned parties informed of what was going on and
to give them avenues for input into the planning process. Getting the job done without incident would be enough for many
superintendents, but not for Townsend. It became clear that
year-round education had to be more than an enrollment-
pressure safety valve. In Townsend's words, "My goal has been to
use this major change as an opportunity to improve education
for students. People are going to have to 'do things differently,' so
how can we do them better? The bottom line for making any and
all decisions has been 'What will be best for the students?'
Satisfying staff is important, but student needs come first." Facing difficult choices, and forced to deal with conflicting views on
issues related to year-round schooling, the bottom line for Rene
Townsend was to emphasize students' welfare.

William D. Greenfield (1991), an influential writer on

moral leadership, concludes from his research that an important source of interpersonal influence among teachers, as between principals and teachers, is their own moral perspectives
and the views they hold of themselves, of their work, and of the
purposes that guide their work. For him, beliefs and ideals
shape practice and engage teachers at the moral level. Following
Etzioni (1964), Greenfield points out that normative power is a
potent and efficient means of cultivating moral involvement on
the part of teachers.

Superintendent Townsend was able to transform a management problem, themed to efficient use of buildings, into a
values problem by connecting it to purposes that had significance for the people involved. When management process and
value substance are joined, new meaning is created, and leadership practice is enriched in terms of values.

Hunter Lewis (1990, p. 12) identifies six modes by which
we arrive at knowledge: "These six modes not only describe how
we think about things in general, they also describe how we
develop and choose values. Some value systems are based on
authority; others are based on deductive logic, sense experience,
emotion, intuition, or science. Over the centuries, for example,
Christianity has often been associated with authority although it
makes a strong emotional, intuitive, and logical appeal as well.
Political candidates' frequently professed values of 'family and
neighborhood' are mostly emotional, and so on. All values and
value systems may be defined in these terms" (p. 12). Lewis
compellingly argues that the six modes of knowing ultimately
determine our personal values and establish within us the value
system that determines what is truth, shapes our choices, and
determines our behavior: "Human beings cannot separate the
way they arrive at values from the values themselves. Authority,
deductive logic, sense experience, emotion, intuition, and science are modes or techniques of moral reasoning but by adopting and emphasizing one over the other we turn them into
dominant personal values" (p. 14).

Lewis defines the six modes as follows:

1. Authority. Taking someone else's word, having
   faith in an external authority. For example,
   having faith in church or Bible.

2. Deductive logic. Subjecting beliefs to the variety of consistency tests that underlie deductive reasoning.
3. Sense experience. Gaining direct knowledge through our own five senses.
4. Emotion. Feeling that something is right: Although we do not usually associate feeling with thinking or judging we actually "think" and "judge" through our emotions all the time.
5. Intuition. Unconscious thinking that is rational rather than emotional. . . . Most creative discoveries are intuitively derived, and only later "dressed up" by logic, observation, or some other conscious technique.
6. "Science." A synthetic technique that relies on sense experience to collect the observable facts; intuition to develop a test of a hypothesis about the facts; logic to develop the test (experiment); and sense experience again to complete the test [pp. 10–12].

Lewis's framework provides the basis for the discussion that follows.

For our purposes, it seems appropriate to differentiate between secular and sacred authority. The term *secular* will refer to the authority of rule or law (as represented in legal codes) and to systems of bureaucratic rules and regulations. The term *sacred* will refer to the authority of religious tracts, the authority of professional or community norms and shared purposes, and the authority of the democratic ideal or other ideals. Codes, rules, and regulations have temporal, objective, and impersonal qualities; tracts, norms, and ideals, by contrast, are decidedly more personal. This differentiation is not without problems, since legal and bureaucratic codes often engender veneration equal to or greater than that accorded to tracts, norms, and ideals. Indeed, one of the reasons for the loss of leadership under the managerial mystique is the veneration with which bureaucratic values are treated in the traditional literature and

Table 1.1. Modes of Knowing as Sources of Official, Semiofficial, and Unofficial Values of Management.

Official	Semiofficial	Unofficial
Secular authority (faith in the authority of the bureaucratic system)	Sense experience (faith in one's experiences)	Sacred authority (faith in the authority of community, professional norms, school norms, and ideals)
Science (faith in the findings of empirical research)	Intuition (faith in one's insight)	Emotions (faith in one's feelings)
Deductive logic (faith in deductive reasoning)		

by many social scientists interested in organizational theory and behavior.

Official and Unofficial Management Values

We can group the modes by which we come to know and believe into three categories: those that are sources for the official values of management, those that are sometimes sources but are not fully recognized (semiofficial), and those that have become unofficial sources. The three groupings are illustrated in Table 1.1.

It is not the purpose of this discussion to choose sides. All modes are legitimate, and all have a place in school management and leadership practice: that is the point. In practice, some are considered legitimate today, but others are not. Sacred authority and emotion are neglected and often ignored; when acknowledged, they are thought to be weak, impressionistic concepts, and more myth than reality—ideas to be avoided, if not scorned. Sense experience and intuition, while acknowledged, do not enjoy equal standing with secular authority, science, and deductive logic. What results from not giving equal attention to all modes is an impoverished management theory and a leadership practice that may not be leadership at all.

Secular authority, science, and deductive logic are al-gorithmic in nature and produce scripts for us to follow. Their claim to fame is "technical rationality," in the form of knowledge considered to be "bigger than we are." As teachers, principals, and superintendents, our place is subordinate to this knowl-edge. When they are used in isolation, secular authority, science, and deductive logic use *us*, in a sense, to achieve their ends, rather than becoming tools that we use to achieve our ends. These modes of knowing become surrogates for the state achieved when the mind and the heart of leadership drive the hand directly. With these official ways of knowing, discretion is reduced or even eliminated. Without discretion, school adminis-trators are not free to decide but only to do, not free to write the script of schools but only to follow the script that someone else provides. Without discretion, in other words, there can be no leadership.

In recent years, sense experience and intuition have made important inroads into legitimacy as modes of knowing. The work on reflective practice within the professions constitutes one noteworthy example of this trend. This work makes a distinction between scientific and professional knowledge, claiming that the latter is created in use as professionals solve problems too indi-vidual for standard recipes. It suggests that traditional ways of knowing — secular authority, science, and deductive logic — should inform but not prescribe practice; knowing comes through acting as professionals research contexts and experi-ment with different courses of action. For Donald Schön (1984), a leader of this movement, reflection in action involves "on-the-spot surfacing, criticizing, re-structuring and testing of intuitive un-derstandings of experience . . . ; often, it takes the form of a reflec-tive conversation with the situation" (p. 42).

Arthur Blumberg (1989), Henry Mintzberg (1987), and others who seek to legitimize the notion of craft as a proper metaphor for the work of leadership have also had an effect on legitimizing sense experience and intuition. Blumberg's re-search (1989, p. 47) has led him to believe that successful prac-tice in school administration requires the development of craft know-how. Such know-how includes the following:

- The ability to develop and refine a "nose" for things
- A sense of what constitutes an acceptable result in any particular problematic situation
- An understanding of the materials with which one is working, including oneself, others, and the environment as it affects the materials and the acceptability of solutions at particular times
- Knowledge of what to do and when to do it, which not only involves pragmatic decisions (what behavior or procedure is called for at a particular time), but also implies issues of right and wrong (see Tom, 1984, on teaching as a moral craft)
- A sense of process — that is, the ability to diagnose and interpret the meaning of what is occurring as people interact in any problematic situation.

With respect to the fourth point, administration is also a practice in which there are moral dimensions to every action taken (with the possible exception of actions that are simply mundane). This is not to suggest, however, that administrators are aware of these moral dimensions at all times; it is simply to suggest that such dimensions are present.

Moral Authority as a Basis of Leadership

While sense experience and intuition have wide currency among practicing managers and leaders in schools, they have much less legitimacy as sources of official management values. Sacred authority and emotion also enjoy wide currency in the world of practice but have virtually no standing within academic conceptions of management, and so the values that emerge from their use are unofficial. From sacred authority come such values as purposing, or building a covenant of shared values, one that bonds people in a common cause and transforms a school from an organization into a community. (These themes will be discussed in later chapters.)

Lewis (1990, p. 87) believes that value systems based on emotion are actually more alike than different; in his view, they share three features. "First, they all focus on a particular group of people, a 'chosen' people, to use the biblical metaphor. Membership in this group automatically provides emotional security. Second, they all propound a particular way of life or a particular way of organizing society, belief in which provides an emotional identity." The third feature is that they all require an emotional stimulus, such as a mission, a sense of purpose, or a covenant of shared values, which represents the core or center that defines the group as a community. Lewis refers to these value systems as "systems of blood."

By giving more credence to sense experience and intuition, and by accepting sacred authority and emotion as fully legitimate ways of knowing, equal in value to secular authority, science, and deductive logic, the value systems undergirding management theory and leadership practice will grow large enough to account for a new kind of leadership — one based on moral authority. This kind of leadership can transform schools into communities and inspire the kind of commitment, devotion, and service that will make our schools unequaled among society's institutions.

But how do we know whether this new kind of leadership will work? The answer lies in the extent to which it is able to tap the human will in a fashion that both motivates and inspires — the topic of the next chapter.

2

What Motivates?
What Inspires?

What kinds of events and circumstances in a typical school day make you feel especially good? What makes you feel lousy? When I asked Catherine Piersall, principal of the San Antonio School, Dade City, Florida, she responded this way:

> The positive feedback and "evidence" of successful decisions make me feel especially good. For example, watching a new program, a new approach, a new teacher, and seeing this situation as being successful, are very rewarding to me. Another example of something that makes me feel good is to hear good reports on "my" students who have left our school and are doing well in other school/life situations—the phone call or comment from a parent who tells me, "Johnny had such problems that year at San An but, thanks to your help, he's doing great now." I feel lousy as a result of the inability to do what I think needs to be done to help a child—the inability to control the situations that lead to inappropriate behavior, learning problems, and the like.

It is hard to find even a hint of self-interest in Piersall's response, nor does she respond as an individual separate from

17

her commitments to the school or the other groups with which
she identifies. Is Catherine Piersall an anomaly? Is there any
reason to believe that what matters to her, including emotions, is
different from what matters to her teachers, to principals, or to
teachers elsewhere?

Underestimating Human Potential

This chapter seeks to understand what motivates us to take one
course of action rather than another. What inspires us to reach
beyond, to give extraordinary effort, to become one with our
work? What is the nature of human reason and will? What
determines our goals, wants, and needs?

In the past, answers to these questions have overplayed the
importance of self-interest, personal pleasure, and individual
choice as driving forces and underplayed more altruistic expla-
nations, such as the extent to which we identify with and are
influenced by membership in groups (church and ethnic
groups, the teaching profession, school communities, social
networks, neighborhoods, our nation). One consequence has
been the development and use of management theory and
leadership practice that underestimate the complexity of
human nature and the capacity of people to be motivated for
reasons other than self-interest.

The problem is that we often lead with the wrong assumptions. For this reason, the yield in commitment and performance is well under what most people are able and willing to
give to their work. This situation will not improve if we merely
try harder to do the same things, fine-tuning current leadership
practices. Improving our yield means changing our outlook.

Etzioni (1988, p. ix) asks, "Are men and women akin to
singleminded, 'cold' calculators, each out to 'maximize' his or
her well-being? Are humans able to figure out rationally the
most efficient way to realize their goals? Is society mainly a
marketplace, in which self-serving individuals compete with
one another — at work, in politics, and in courtship — enhancing
the general welfare in the process? Or do we typically seek to do
both what is right *and* what is pleasurable, and find ourselves

frequently in conflict when moral values and happiness are incompatible?"

The prevailing view in management and motivation theory, a view borrowed from classical economic theory, assumes that human beings are by nature selfish. They are driven by a desire to maximize self-interest and thus continually calculate courses of action and the benefits of various options, choosing the actions that will either make them winners or keep them from losing. In this thinking, self-interest is so dominant that love, loyalty, outrage, obligation, duty, goodness, dedication, and desire to help count very little in determining why we do what we do. Emotions are considered a form of currency that one uses to get something. A loving relationship, for example, is little more than a contract within which two people exchange sentiments and commitments to gain benefits less easily available outside the relationship. Work relationships and commitments are seen as stemming from even more selfish urges.

The Importance of Moral Judgment

In providing an alternative to the view that self-interest is the prime motivator, Etzioni (1988) assumes that human beings pass moral judgments on their own urges. To a large extent, moral commitments explain the decisions people make and the behavior they exhibit. The pitting of self-interest against moral judgment resembles the ancient (and still current) debate in philosophy between deontologists and utilitarians. Deontologists put most of their money on moral judgment as the prime motivator. Utilitarians bet on self-interest.

The position of the utilitarians has two dimensions. The first is *individual* self-interest. As individuals, we do the things that provide us with the greatest gain or help us incur the smallest loss. The second dimension, too often overlooked in management theory and leadership practice, is self-interest *broadly conceived*: we seek to maximize not only our individual self-interest but also that of the commonweal, to enhance whatever promotes the general welfare, in the belief that it ultimately contributes to our own. In the long run, it is in the individual's interest to promote the common good. Understood in this way, utilitarianism reveals an important dimension of developing a moral outlook on leadership, one in which the interests of the commonweal become primary and the elevation of self-interest raises moral questions.

The roots of deontology are long, but Immanuel Kant's philosophy seems best to summarize this viewpoint for our purposes. In his classical treatise *Foundation of the Metaphysics of Morals* ([1785] 1959), Kant maintains that any action, in order to be moral, must be taken in the belief and because of the belief that it is right—from duty, not because of personal inclination, gain, or love.

Moral Judgment and Motivation

What motivates? What inspires? People answer these questions according to which of the three views—selfish utilitarianism, commonweal utilitarianism, or deontology—or which combination of them they identify with. Is your bottom line individual self-interest? When it comes to motivating teachers, students, parents, and others, is only what gets rewarded what gets done? Or do you believe that people are capable of seeing their fate as connected to their various memberships (family, neighborhood, workplace, community, religious groups, and nation)? Is it your view that when individual self-interest and commonweal self-interest are in conflict we can sacrifice the former for the sake of the latter? Do you believe that we are capable of responding first to the duties and obligations that stand above self-interest of any kind? Are we, as Kant suggests, morally responsive?

These questions raise still others. Is the individual the decision-making unit and therefore free to make independent decisions? Or do you assume, as Etzioni does, that "social collectivities (such as ethnic and racial groups, peer groups at work, and neighborhood groups) are the prime decision-making units" (1988, p. 4)? Etzioni acknowledges that individual decision making does exist but that it typically reflects collective attributes and processes, since decisions are made in the context

created by people's memberships in various groups. Our connections are so important, and the process of socialization that
implicitly or explicitly takes place as a result of our memberships in and identification with groups is so complete, that
the notion of the individual decision maker, so dominant in
traditional management theory and leadership practice, is
more myth than reality.

The position argued here is that we humans regularly pass
moral judgments on our individual urges and routinely sacrifice
our self-interest and pleasure. Indeed, a Gallup poll revealed
that 91 percent of respondents agreed with the statement "Duty
comes before pleasure," and only 3 percent disagreed (Gallup
Organization, 1988). Our actions and decisions are influenced
by what we value and believe, as well as by self-interest. When the
two are in conflict, values and beliefs usually take precedence.

What Is Important to Teachers?

What does the evidence suggest? What is important to teachers
at work? What motivates them? What inspires them? What keeps
them going even when the going gets tough?

Let's examine some of the evidence. The sociologist Dan
Lortie (1975), in his landmark study of teachers in Dade County,
Florida, asked his respondents what attracted them to teaching.
The themes that dominated their responses were serving others,
working with people (particularly students), enjoyment of the
job itself, material benefits, and the school calendar.

More recently, Susan Moore Johnson (1990) asked similar
questions in her interview study of 115 Massachusetts public,
private, and religious school teachers. Here are examples of the
responses:

> The way you could just look into a kid's eyes, the
> sparkle when you showed them something that they
> didn't know or that they couldn't understand. . . .
> There was an energy there that was quite gratifying.
> It made me want to keep coming back [p. 34].

There was something that always attracted me to
teaching. I just feel like this is my profession. My
bottom line is that I love kids. I get energy from
them. I just think they're the brightest people on
earth [p. 34].

No special reason. I was interested in language. I
guess that would be the reason. I started off in
Spanish. I thought that teaching would be the best
way to make use of what I was studying, because I
enjoyed it [p. 36].

I feel that God has given all of us a gift to do
something. Everybody has a strength. I really believe this strongly, that I can give children education, make them feel good about themselves, let
them learn to like to read, let them look at school as
Wow! This is wonderful [p. 37].

The dominant themes that emerged from Johnson's research
were working with students; an interest in the intellectual processes, puzzles, problems, and challenges of pedagogy as an
occupation; a commitment to learning more or being more fully
engaged in a particular subject area or discipline; social purposes, in the sense of making a difference in society; religious
purposes, in the sense of being called to the "ministry" of teaching; and a convenient calendar that allowed the combination of
a career with a family, or of a career with other life interests,
mostly themed to personal development.

Johnson points out that the rewards of teaching do not
come cheaply:

Despite the teachers' successes with children and
their satisfactions with a school schedule that made
it possible for many of them to work, they reported
frustration and disappointment. Both originated
primarily from conditions found in the workplace
of teaching. Throughout the interviews teachers

from both the public and private sectors characterized this unsteady balance between assets and
deficits. One public elementary school teacher
said, "I get satisfaction, I get a lot of love from the
kids I teach. I really feel that I have the possibility to
make a difference in somebody's life, which to me is
worth more than money, I guess. I mean, certainly
you're not in it for the money. And you're not in it
for the prestige. And you're not in it for the sense of
autonomy you have, because you don't have much
autonomy, in terms of what you want to do. But for
what you get from the one-on-one with kids, I don't
think anyone could replace that feeling for me
personally" [Johnson; 1990, p. 42].

The teachers in Johnson's study reported few rewards
beyond those gained by working with students and from other
aspects of the work itself. For example, they were dissatisfied
with low pay, lack of respect, few opportunities for advancement, lack of administrative support, unnecessary bureaucratic
demands, poorly maintained buildings, nonteaching duties,
lack of parental involvement, limited autonomy, isolation from
other teachers, and the lack of a voice in governance and decision making. It appears from Johnson's research that calling,
sense of mission, and commitment to professional, social, or
religious ideals are important enough to carry teachers, despite
the difficulties they encounter in the schools. Clearly, individual
self-interest counts in motivating these teachers, but so does
commonweal self-interest and a sense of what is morally good.
(These findings raise another set of moral questions. Some
people, for example, are happy to exploit the fact that many
teachers are so motivated by practicing a policy of neglect.)

The evidence seems clear: self-interest is not powerful
enough to account fully for human motivation. We are also
driven by what we believe is right and good, by how we feel about
things, and by the norms that emerge from our connections
with other people; we are driven, to use Etzioni's terms, by
morality, emotion, and social bonds, which together comprise

the assumptions that underlie a morally based leadership. Human beings pass moral judgments on their individual urges. As a result, they often sacrifice self-interest for the sake of other causes and reasons. People choose largely on the basis of preferences and emotions. As members of social groups, they find that their memberships singularly shape their individual decisions.

The Traditional Motivation Rule

The assumptions underlying much of today's leadership practice lead to the embodiment of a very simple motivational rule: What gets rewarded gets done. Motivational experts dispute just how true this rule is. For example, the famous "felt-tip marker" research of David Greene and Mark Lepper (1974) is often cited as evidence that this traditional rule can backfire with children. In that research, preschoolers, who were highly motivated to draw with felt-tip markers when no extrinsic rewards were offered, showed much less interest in the activity after rewards were introduced. Perhaps best known on this theme is the ongoing research of Edward Deci and Richard Ryan (1985). They found that the capacity to be motivated lessened in light of extrinsic rewards and that people working for rewards tended to feel controlled by them. This feeling in turn affected subsequent performance and creativity.

Where the traditional rule can be applied, it appears that people work for rewards, rather than for the sake of the work itself. This finding raises two important questions: What happens when rewards are not available? What happens to other sources of motivation once intrinsic rewards are introduced?

The answer to the first question is that although what gets rewarded often gets done, the reverse is also likely to be true: what does not get rewarded does not get done. In other words, the rule focuses one's attention and narrows one's response to work. Further, for the rule to be sustained, a busy kind of leadership is required. Leaders must constantly monitor the exchange of rewards for work, guess which rewards are of interest to workers and which are not, and figure out ways to keep this exchange going. As a result, workers become increasingly dependent on rewards and on their leaders to motivate them. "What gets rewarded gets done" discourages people from becoming self-managed and self-motivated.

The answer to the second question is equally ominous. "What gets rewarded gets done" can alter one's attachment to an activity, making it extrinsic instead of intrinsic or moral. Imagine, for example, a school that does not specify the exact hours of work. Teachers are expected to do their work and do it well, and it is believed that they are capable of defining their own workdays. Most of the teachers rarely leave the school before 5 P.M.—a full two hours after the students leave. They stay because, on the one hand, they find the work interesting and derive satisfaction from doing a good job and, on the other, because they feel a sense of obligation and duty to their students—for intrinsic and moral reasons. Two of the teachers consistently leave five minutes after the students leave. The administration perceives their early departure from the school grounds as a problem. Consequently, they issue a rule requiring all teachers to stay until 3:30, rewarding those who do and punishing those who do not. After a short time, the vast majority of teachers now leave at or shortly after 3:30.

What has happened in this case? The explanation is partly attributable to a change in the teachers' attachment to their work. Once they were involved for intrinsic and moral reasons; now they are involved for calculated reasons. "A fair day's work for a fair day's pay" has been defined for them, and a reward system has been established on the basis of this definition. The tendency now is for teachers to calculate, very carefully, the proper equation of investment in work, to match payoffs received in return. They are now, in other words, involved for extrinsic rather than intrinsic and moral reasons.

When calculated involvement is combined with narrowed focus, the ingredients for sustained superior performance are effectively removed. As the distinguished organizational theorist James G. March (1984) points out, "Long before reaching the top, an intelligent manager learns that some of the more effective ways of improving measured performance have little to do with improving product, service or technology. A system of

rewards linked to precise measures is not an incentive to perform well; it is an incentive to obtain a good score" (pp. 27–28).
March's observations raise nagging questions about the consequences of the strategies now being used to motivate students.

The traditional motivational rule—"What gets rewarded
gets done"—has its place, but by itself it is neither powerful nor
expansive enough to provide the kind of motivational climate
needed in schools. One alternative to this rule is "What is
rewarding gets done." The work gets done, and it gets done
without close supervision or other controls. The sources of
motivation are embedded in the work itself.

Frederick Herzberg (1966) has pointed out that jobs in
which there are opportunities for and feelings of achievement
and responsibility, jobs that offer interesting and challenging
work and opportunities for advancement, have the greatest
capacity to motivate. These are not factors that leaders can give
to others in return for desired behavior; they are an integral part
of the work itself. Herzberg's research and that of others builds a
case for the idea that what is rewarding gets done. Such research
has shown that jobs with the following characteristics enhance
intrinsic motivation:

> Allow for discovery, exploration, variety and chal-
> lenge. Provide high involvement with the task and
> high identity with the task, enabling work to be
> considered important and significant. Allow for
> active participation. Emphasize agreement with re-
> spect to broad purposes and values that bond peo-
> ple together at work. Permit outcomes within
> broad purposes to be determined by the worker.
> Encourage autonomy and self-determination. Al-
> low persons to feel like "origins" of their own behav-
> ior rather than "pawns" manipulated from the out-
> side. Encourage feelings of competence and
> control and enhance feelings of efficacy [Ser-
> giovanni, 1990, p. 129].

There is a conversation in management theory supporting the idea that what is rewarding gets done, but there is virtual

Table 2.1. Three Rules of Motivation.

Rule	Motivation	Involvement
What gets rewarded gets done	Extrinsic gain	Calculated
What is rewarding gets done	Intrinsic gain	Intrinsic
What is good gets done	Duty or obligation	Moral

silence on a second alternative rule: What we believe in, and what we feel obligated to do because of a moral commitment, gets done. Again, it gets done, and it gets done well, without close supervision or other controls. One purpose of this book is to advance this motivational rule to a position at least equal to that of the other two. (The three are summarized in Table 2.1.)

Authenticity

Assumptions underlying traditional leadership practice (self-interest, the separation of emotion from fact, the notion of freestanding individuals) help people feel safe. In practice, however, they form an abstract, antiseptic view of management and leadership.

The view proposed in this book is more authentic in a psychological sense and more real in its consequences for leadership. We often hide by going through a Jekyll-to-Hyde metamorphosis on the way to work each morning, only to change back to our real selves on the way home. The result is guarded behavior, an abstract approach to problems and issues, and a tendency to solve problems superficially. By contrast, a moral perspective on leadership can help us stop "playing school" and start "living school" more authentically.

When Irwin Blumer was executive director of curriculum and instruction for the Concord and Concord–Carlisle (Massachusetts) School District, he established an administrative council that consisted of all the district's principals, central office staff members, and curriculum coordinators. The purpose of the council was to discuss issues vital to the school district and make recommendations for policy and programs. Initially, Blumer says, the council's discussions were "cursory and nonproductive. This was not related to a lack of commitment. The problem with our discussions stemmed from the esoteric, abstract nature of the comments and our inability to pinpoint specific needs and possible next steps."

The issues being discussed were respect for individual differences and the value of integrating minority students more fully into the school community. The director of social work for the district said she would be willing to help plan an administrative council meeting that would allow each participant to examine the issues from his or her own perspective. Blumer explains, "At that meeting, she and several other administrators delved into their past experiences, in an attempt to help all of us feel comfortable sharing and learning from our own differences. This set the tone for each of us to describe our own experiences and differences. We talked about where we grew up; the kinds of families that we came from; our aspirations as children, young adults, and mature adults; our relationships with our parents and children; and the effect of our religion or race upon our own development. What started as a two-hour meeting extended to three hours, and then to several fairly long sessions, before we were able to complete the process."

Blumer reports that the process was beneficial because it allowed members of the administrative council to gain a better perspective on others in the group and to begin knowing one another as people, rather that just as fellow employees. He remarks, "Since I was a newcomer to the district, I was not surprised that I knew little about staff members' backgrounds. However, I was shocked to learn that people who had literally worked together for twenty years had the same level of knowledge about each other that I did. The force of the experience was so great that several of the principals discussed this project with their own staffs. As a result, some staff members asked for a similar kind of sharing experience, using faculty meeting time. The results were as powerful as those we experienced."

Blumer's story suggests that, deep down, we know what motivates and what inspires, but to tap these sources of motivation more fully we must embark on a journey to make school life more meaningful. Our emotions need to become legitimate.

We need to be in touch with our basic values and with our connections to others. In other words, we must become more authentic with ourselves and others. If we are successful, we will be able to transform schools from ordinary organizations into learning communities. But success will mean seeking new bases of authority for leadership. Bureaucratic and psychological leadership are not enough. Our goal should be to develop a leadership practice based on professional and moral authority—the topic of the next chapter.

3

The Sources of Authority
for Leadership

Whom should one follow? What should one follow? Why should one follow? In traditional management, *whom* means the designated leader anointed from above or commissioned by the institution. *What* is the leader's vision or, in its absence, the leader's or institution's script. The answer to *why* is that the leader is able to coax compliance through deft interpersonal skill or has the clout to command it.

Leaders prefer that the led do not ask "why" questions. If an explanation were forced, it might be something like this: "Follow me because of my position in the school and the system of roles, expectations, and rules that I represent." This is the simplest and most direct way to get things done in school: rely on bureaucratic authority. Bureaucratic authority exists in the form of mandates, rules, regulations, job descriptions, and expectations. When we base our leadership practice on bureaucratic authority, teachers respond appropriately or face the consequences.

An alternative response might be "Follow me because I will make it worth your while if you do." This is perhaps the most popular way to get things done in schools: rely on psychological authority. Psychological authority is expressed in the form of motivational technology and human relations skills. When we base our leadership practice on psychological authority, teachers are supposed to respond to our personality, and to the pleasant environment that we provide, by behaving appropriately and collecting the rewards we make available.

Still another response might be "Follow me because I have been trained in the research and know what is best, as determined by this research." This approach has gained popularity in recent years, as a result of the emphasis on principals' being instructional leaders and basing their practice on teaching-effectiveness research or school-effectiveness research: in other words, rely on technical-rational authority. Technical-rational authority exists in the form of evidence derived from logic and scientific research. When we base our leadership practice on such authority, we expect teachers to respond in light of what is considered to be true.

"Follow me" is so much a part of our thinking that we often miss the whole point of leadership. The true leader is one who builds in substitutes for "follow me" leadership, which enable people to respond from within. "Follow me" leadership cannot work without some external force that pushes or pulls people in a desired direction. Further, "follow me" always requires follow-up in the form of monitoring, to ensure that the desired movement continues. "Follow me" leadership, in other words, is management-intensive. Skillfully practiced, it often gets people to cooperate, but it cannot inspire the kind of commitment that will make schools work and work well, because it tends to induce a state of subordination among teachers, rather than followership (a theme that will be explored in later chapters).

There are two other sources of authority on which to base leadership practice. Neither one is management- or leadership-intensive, and both create a response in teachers that comes from within, rather than being imposed.

One source is professional authority, in the form of seasoned craft knowledge and personal expertise. When leadership practice is based on professional authority, teachers can be expected to respond to common socialization, accepted tenets of practice, and internalized expertise.

The other source is moral authority, in the form of obligations and duties derived from widely shared values, ideas, and ideals. When leadership practice is based on moral authority, teachers can be expected to respond to shared commitments and felt interdependence.

Five sources of authority for leadership—with lists of assumptions, implications for practice, and consequences for schools—are shown in Table 3.1. Each of the five is legitimate and should be part of the basis of authority for leadership practice, but it makes a difference which source or combination of sources is primary. Primary authority for today's leadership rests in a combination of bureaucratic, psychological, and technical-rational sources.

If we were to add professional and moral authority to bureaucratic, psychological, and technical-rational sources, and if those two became the *primary* sources of authority for leadership, the "why" questions would be answered differently. To begin with, the order of the questions would change. We would begin with *what* to follow: the shared values and beliefs that define us as a community, and the ideals that define us as professionals. Then we would ask *why*: because it is morally right to do so; community and professional memberships are morally understood as duties and obligations. And *whom* should we follow? Ourselves as members and as morally conscious, committed people.

Most readers probably have little difficulty accepting the assertion that bureaucratic leadership is overemphasized in schools; most of the related assumptions listed in Table 3.1 are too suspect. For example, few believe that most teachers are not trustworthy and do not share the same goals and interests as administrators do. Even fewer would accept the idea that hierarchy equals expertise. The remaining assumptions—that teachers are subordinates in a hierarchically arranged system, and that external monitoring works best—would perhaps be less contested. Maybe that is why much of school leadership relies on "expect and inspect," predetermined standards, inservice, and direct supervision. Those assumptions also explain why school administrators seem to spend so much time trying to figure out how to motivate teachers, and what change strategies to use in making them do things differently.

Nevertheless, it is another matter to suggest that psychological leadership is overdone, and that relying excessively on psychology as a source of authority has negative consequences for teachers and students. Most school administrators tend to see knowledge and skill about how to motivate, apply the correct leadership style, boost morale, and engineer the right interpersonal climate as representing the heart of what school administration is — the "core technology" of the educational administration profession. After all, these are the concerns that typically dominate school administration curricula, loom large on lists of administrative proficiencies, and are highly prized when administrators are hired. The fact that psychologically based leadership is important is not being challenged here, but that it should enjoy such prominence is challenged.

The view argued in this book is that psychological leadership, along with leadership based on bureaucratic authority and technical-rational authority, has a place but that its place should be to provide support for professional and moral authority. The latter two should be the primary bases for leadership practice.

Why should leadership based on psychological know-how and skill not be a primary source of authority for school leadership? One reason, already discussed in Chapter Two, is that psychological leadership cannot tap the full range and depth of human capacity and will. It cannot elicit the kind of motivated, spirited response from parents, teachers, and students that will allow schools to work well and students to become fully functioning persons.

Another reason is that, practically and morally, there are better motives for teachers', students', and parents' involvement than the leader's personality or psychological rewards. Emil J. Haller and Kenneth Strike (1986, p. 326) believe that the administrator's building expertise around interpersonal themes raises serious ethical questions:

> We find this an inadequate view of the administrative role. . . its first deficiency is that it makes administrative success depend on characteristics that tend to be both intangible and unalterable. One person's dynamic leader is another's tyrant. What one person sees as a democratic style, an-

other will see as the generation of time-wasting committee work... our basic concern with this view, however, is that it makes the administrative role one of form, not content. Being a successful administrator depends not on the adequacy of one's view, not on the educational policies that one adopts and how reasonable they are, and not on how successful one is in communicating these reasons to others. Success depends on personality and style, or on carefully chosen ways of inducing others to contribute to the organization. It is not what one wants to do and why that is important; it is who one is and how one does things that counts. We find such a view offensive. It is incompatible with the values of autonomy, reason and democracy, which we see among the central commitments of our society and our educational system. Of course educational administrators must be leaders, but let them stand by reason and persuasion, not by forces of personality.

Haller and Strike's perspective raises troubling questions. What are the reasons why you should follow the lead of your supervisors? Because they know how to manipulate? Because they can meet your needs or provide you with other psychological payoffs? Because they are charming and fun to be with? Or because they have something to say that makes sense? Because their thoughts point you in a direction that captures your imagination? Because they stand on ideas, values, and conceptions that you believe are good for teachers, students, and the school?

The question is, Do we choose between glitz or substance? Bennis (1989, p. 160) puts his finger on the problem: "Once we believed that success was achieved through hard work, frugality, industry, diligence, prudence, and honesty. Now we believe that success is based on our personality alone. If we can please other people, we will succeed. Instead of working at work, we work on our personalities. Instead of being good at what we do, we opt for charm. And we do not dream, we fantasize."

Proposing that a psychologically based leadership practice is dysfunctionally overplayed in schools may raise concerns,
but suggesting that technical-rational authority is equally dys-
functional may be considered heresy. After all, we live in a
society where what is scientific is prized. Given our deference to
science, our first glance at the assumptions and related practices
underlying the authority of technical-rationality (see Table 3.1)
is likely to elicit a nod of agreement. But teaching and learning
are too complex to be captured so simply. In the real world,
none of those assumptions hold up very well, and the related
practices portray an antiseptic view of teaching, supervision,
and school leadership.

There is a growing sense among researchers, teachers,
and policy analysts that the context for teaching practice is too
idiosyncratic, nonlinear, and loosely connected for simplistic
conceptions of teaching to work (Lieberman, 1988; Sergiovanni,
1989; Darling-Hammond and Sclam, forthcoming). Teaching
cannot be standardized. Like other professionals, teachers cannot become effective by following scripts. Instead, they need to
create *knowledge in use* as they practice—becoming skilled surfers who ride the wave of the pattern of teaching (Sergiovanni,
1987). This ability requires a higher level of reflection, understanding, and skill than that offered in the guise of technical-
rational authority.

While technical-rational authority for leadership practice
has some similarity to the authority of professionalism (both, for
example, rely on expertise), technical-rational authority assumes that the expertness of knowledge itself is primary, and
that such knowledge exists apart from the context of teaching:
the job of the teacher is simply to apply knowledge to practice,
and the teacher is subordinate to the knowledge base of
teaching.

Professional authority as a basis for leadership assumes
that the expertise of teachers is what counts most. Knowledge
does not exist apart from teacher and context, and so teachers
are always superordinate to the knowledge base. They use
knowledge metaphorically, to inform but not to prescribe practice. In the professions, knowledge of theory and research is not

Table 3.1. The Sources of Authority for Leadership/Supervisory Policy and Practice.

Source	Assumptions When Use of This Source is Primary	Leadership/Supervisory Strategy	Consequences
Bureaucratic authority			
Hierarchy	Teachers are subordinates in a hierarchically arranged system.	"Expect and inspect" is the overarching rule.	With proper monitoring, teachers respond as technicians, executing predetermined scripts, and their performance is narrowed.
Rules and regulations	Supervisors are trustworthy, but subordinates are not.	Rely on predetermined standards, to which teachers must measure up.	
Mandates			
Role expectation	Goals and interests of teachers and supervisors are not the same, and supervisors must be watchful.	Identify their needs and "inservice" them.	
(Teachers comply or face consequences.)			
	Hierarchy equals expertise, and so supervisors know more than teachers do.	Directly supervise and closely monitor the work of teachers, to ensure compliance.	
	External accountability works best.	Figure out how to motivate them and get them to change.	
Psychological authority			
Motivation technology	The goals and interests of teachers and supervisors are not the same but can be bartered so that each side gets what it wants.	Develop a school climate characterized by high congeniality among teachers and between teachers and supervisors.	Teachers respond as required when rewards are available, but not otherwise; their involvement is calculated and performance is narrowed.
Interpersonal skills			
Human relations			
Leadership	Teachers have needs, and if they are met at work, the work gets done as required.	"Expect and reward."	
(Teachers will want to comply because of the congenial climate and the rewards.)			

	Congenial relationships and a harmonious interpersonal climate make teachers content, easier to work with, and more apt to cooperate.	"What gets rewarded gets done."	With proper monitoring, teachers respond as technicians, executing predetermined steps; performance is narrowed.
	Supervisors must be experts in reading needs and in other people-handling skills, to barter successfully for compliance and increases in performance.	Use psychological authority in combination with bureaucratic and technical-rational authority.	
Technical-rational authority	Supervision and teaching are applied sciences.	Use research, to identify best practice.	
Evidence defined by logic and scientific research	Knowledge of research is privileged.	Standardize the work of teaching, to reflect the best way.	
(Teachers are required to comply in light of what is considered to be the truth.)	Scientific knowledge is superordinate to practice.	"Inservice" teachers in the best way.	
	Teachers are skilled technicians.	Monitor the process, to ensure compliance.	
	Values, preferences, and beliefs do not count, but facts and objective evidence do.	Figure out ways to motivate them and get them to change.	

Table 3.1. The Sources of Authority for Leadership/Supervisory Policy and Practice, Cont'd.

Source	Assumptions When Use of This Source is Primary	Leadership/Supervisory Strategy	Consequences
Professional authority			
Informed craft knowledge and personal expertise (Teachers respond in light of common socialization, professional values, accepted tenets of practice, and internalized expertise.)	Situations of practice are idiosyncratic, and no one best way exists.	Promote a dialogue among teachers that explicitly states professional values and accepted tenets of practice.	Teachers respond to professional norms; their practice becomes collective, they require little monitoring, and their performance is expansive.
	Scientific knowledge and professional knowledge are different, with professional knowledge created in use as teachers practice.	Translate them into professional standards.	
	The purpose of scientific knowledge is to inform, not prescribe, practice.	Give teachers as much discretion as they want and need.	
	Authority cannot be external but comes from the context itself and from within the teacher.	Require teachers to hold one another accountable for meeting practice standards.	
	Authority from context comes from training and experience.	Make assistance, support, and professional development opportunities available.	
	Authority from within comes from socialization and internalized values.		

Moral authority

Felt obligation and duties derived from widely shared community values, ideas, and ideals (Teachers respond to shared commitments and felt interdependence.)	Schools are professional learning communities. Communities are defined by their centers of shared values, beliefs, and commitments. In communities, what is considered right and good is as important as what works and what is effective; people are motivated as much by emotion and beliefs as by self-interest; and collegiality is a professional virtue.	Identify and make explicit the values and beliefs that define the center of the school as a community. Translate them into informal norms that govern behavior. Promote collegiality as internally felt and morally driven interdependence. Rely on the ability of community members to respond to duties and obligations. Rely on the community's informal norms to enforce professional and community values.	Teachers respond to community values for moral reasons; their practice becomes collective, and their performance is expansive and sustained.

considered privileged, and what counts is also what is thought right and good. When there is conflict, knowledge yields. Physicians, for example, do not practice treatments just because they work; treatments must also meet the standards of good practice and the profession's accepted values and norms. Professional authority is a very powerful force for governing what teachers do. For it to take hold, however, we need to increase our investment in teacher preparation, professional development, and other efforts to upgrade teaching.

The work of the National Board for Professional Teaching Standards provides us with a vision of what teaching can become, once it is professionalized. The board's goal is to raise teaching to the status of the more established professions, in the belief that this will be a practical, effective way to improve learning in our schools over the long term. The board hopes to achieve its goal by establishing high, rigorous standards for what teachers should know and be able to do; teachers who met those standards would become certified. The kind of teacher the board envisions is shown in Exhibit 3.1.

If we can harness the power of professionalism, professional authority will become a driving force for leadership practice. Instead of relying on rules, personality, or interpersonal skills, leaders will be able to rely on standards of practice and professional norms as reasons for doing things. Leadership itself will become less direct and intense as standards and norms take hold.

Many will wonder whether teachers can handle being treated as professionals. Will they accept the extra burden of responsibility and accountability that inevitably goes along with expanded discretion and rights? There is reason to be optimistic, for enough school districts are now making serious efforts to build professionalism, with positive results. In the Shoreham–Wading River Central School District, in New York, teachers are deeply involved in decision making. Assistant superintendent Martin Brooks explains, "Our district historically has been one in which teachers have shared power and responsibility. They develop their own budgets; select and order their own materials; participate in the hiring of all new staff, includ-

Exhibit 3.1. Harnessing the Power of Professionalism: Propositions from the National Board for Professional Teaching Standards.

Our work is based on five fundamental propositions:

Teachers are committed to students and their learning. Board-certified teachers are dedicated to the belief that all students can learn, and that knowledge should be accessible to all of them. They treat students equitably, taking into account each one's uniqueness and structuring their teaching methods accordingly.

Teachers know the subjects they teach, and how to teach those subjects to students. Board-certified teachers thoroughly understand the subjects they teach, and appreciate how knowledge in those subjects is created, organized, linked to other disciplines, and applied to real-world settings.

These teachers command specialized knowledge of how to convey a subject to their students. Their instructional repertoire also makes them adept at teaching students how to analyze and solve their own problems.

Teachers are responsible for managing and monitoring student learning. Board-certified teachers create, enrich, maintain, or alter instructional settings, to capture and sustain the interest of their students while using time effectively.

They know how to engage groups of students, to ensure a disciplined learning environment, and how to organize instruction to allow the school's goals to be met. Accomplished teachers can also assess the progress of individual students and clearly explain students' performance to parents.

Teachers think systematically about their practice and learn from experience. Board-certified teachers exemplify the virtues they seek to inspire in students: curiosity, tolerance, honesty, fairness, respect for diversity, and appreciation of cultural differences.

They also possess the abilities that are prerequisites for intellectual growth: the ability to reason and take multiple perspectives, to be creative and take risks, and to approach problems in an open and systematic manner.

Drawing on their knowledge of human development, subject matter, and instruction, these teachers know their students well enough to make principled judgments about sound teaching methods.

Teachers are members of learning communities. Board-certified teachers contribute to the effectiveness of the school by working collaboratively with other professionals on instructional policy, as well as on curriculum and staff development. They find ways to include parents as essential partners in the learning process. They know about the specialized school and community resources available for their students' benefit and are skilled at employing these resources when needed.

Source: The National Board for Professional Teaching Standards. Summarized from *Education Week*, vol. 10, no. 11, Nov. 14, 1990, p. 23. Reprinted with permission from the board.

ing administrators; collaboratively make curriculum decisions (there are no department chairs or district curriculum coordinators); handle the student placement process; and develop the schools' master schedules." Teachers in the Shoreham–Wading River District also assume responsibility for conducting their own staff development courses and workshops.

We have many professionals in teaching today, but teaching still awaits professional status of the kind envisioned by the National Board for Professional Teaching Standards. The reality is that building professional authority as a source for leadership is a long-term proposition. In the meantime, we can do much to advance leadership by moving moral authority — the authority of felt obligations and duties derived from widely shared professional and community values, ideas, and ideals — to center stage. To accomplish this goal, we must direct our efforts to creating learning communities in each school. The norms and values associated with professionalism, as well as the norms and values that define the school as a learning community, can then become substitutes for leadership, the theme of the next chapter.

4

Substitutes for Leadership

In the last chapter, it was pointed out that the true school leader is one who builds substitutes for "follow me" leadership that enable people to respond from within. Although thinking about substitutes for leadership is not a new idea, it is a radical one. With few exceptions—for example, Philip Selznick's (1957) work on institutional leadership, and Terrence Deal's (1985) work on symbolic leadership—leadership is viewed exclusively as something interpersonal. To have leadership, you need to have a person who will lead and others who will somehow tag along. Leadership has to do with the leader's working directly to get others to do what she or he wants and, if skillful, getting them to enjoy doing it.

Interpersonal leadership is important, but it gives us only part of the picture. If anything, interpersonal leadership represents an early stage, whose ultimate result is a shift of attention away from the leader and to something else. When this "something else" is in place, interpersonal leadership becomes less important. In schools, this means that, instead of worrying constantly about setting the direction and then engaging teachers and others in a successful march (often known as planning, organizing, leading, motivating, and controlling), the "leader" can focus more on removing obstacles, providing material and emotional support, taking care of the management details that make any journey easier, sharing in the comradeship of the march and in the celebration when the journey is completed, and identifying a new, worthwhile destination for the next march. The march takes care of itself.

Valjeane Olenn, principal of Wells High School, Wells, Maine, describes this "evolving leadership" as follows:

> A school needs to be a place where adults, too, can grow and change and learn. The only way a principal can survive in a growth-oriented environment is to relinquish control in many areas and let people work in their own ways. In the end, to relinquish control by allowing others to make decisions and solve problems actually enhances a principal's power. I do not yet sufficiently understand the phenomenon to be able to explain it, but I know that it is so and it is a relief to recognize it. Of course, one does not give up all control; what one does is carefully choose where one needs to exert control. When people are involved in solving their own problems and working out their ideas, a school has a rich body of creative energy to draw upon. The principal has the freedom to spend his or her time helping to develop and direct that energy toward ends that count.

Responsiveness to the norms of school as a learning community, commitment to the professional ideal, responsiveness to the work itself, and collegiality (understood as professional virtue) are four examples of substitutes for leadership. Together, they can provide teachers and others who work in schools with the kind of inspiration, meaning, and motivation that come from within. In other words, there is less need for principals and superintendents to motivate people from the outside by bartering psychological and physical need fulfillment in exchange for compliance. The substitutes for leadership do not eliminate our physical and psychological needs, which still must be met—but not in exchange for anything. Needs should be met because that is the right thing to do, not because we want to get people to do certain things. Further, with the substitutes in place, teachers and others are better able to get their needs met on their own as they engage in the work of the school. This development in turn can take pressure off administrators, allowing them to rechannel their energies.

Not all four substitutes lend themselves equally to the influence of school leaders. Building norms and providing opportunities for teachers and others to experience intrinsic satisfaction in work are bottom-up propositions. They become established from within individual schools and are amenable to ready influence by principals and superintendents. By contrast, promoting the professional ideal requires effort that involves legislators, professional associations, and the public at large. Nevertheless, principals, superintendents, and other school administrators have an important role to play in promoting the ideal locally. In this chapter, we examine community norms and the professional ideal. The work itself is discussed in Chapter Five, and collegiality is discussed in Chapter Seven.

Community Norms as a Substitute for Leadership

Establishing community norms within the school can serve as a substitute for direct leadership. Doing so involves changing the metaphor for schooling: from the image of an instructional delivery system, a factory, batch processing, an organization, a clinical setting, a market, or a garden to that of a *community*. Metaphors are important, for they frame the way we think about managing, leading, and schooling, and they create the reality that we ultimately live as school leaders.

Consider, for example, the image of schooling created by thinking of schools as instructional delivery systems. Your thoughts probably revolve around the following themes:

- How to identify and carefully develop the targets, goals, steps, procedures, timetables, and schedules that will become the basis of establishing the best routes for delivering instruction
- How to train deliverers properly and then provide them with clear instructions for what to do

- How to develop a system of monitoring, to ensure that instruction is delivered properly
- How to provide additional training, to correct mistakes and align what deliverers do with what they are supposed to do
- How to establish an evaluation scheme that measures the extent to which the system is working.

Although known by other names, these are the issues that too often dominate the concerns of today's school leaders.

Instructional delivery systems are designed to be larger than people. They reduce discretion and force administrators and teachers to assume the narrow role of script followers. In these circumstances, what people do depends on external motivation and monitoring. For this reason, instructional delivery systems are management- and leadership-intensive.

If the image changes to that of a learning community, however, the issues that come to mind are likely to be very different. For example, we may be concerned with the following:

- How the learning community will be defined
- What the relationships will be among parents, students, teachers, and administrators if the school is to become a community
- What shared values, purposes, and commitments bond the community
- How parents, teachers, administrators, and students will work together to embody these values
- What kinds of obligations to the community members should have and how these will be enforced.

The image of a learning community suggests a very different kind of leadership practice from that found in an instructional delivery system. What is true changes as we change our metaphor for schooling.

It is common to speak of schools in the language of culture. Edgar H. Schein (1985), a respected authority on the subject, points out that culture refers to "the deeper level of *basic assumptions* and *beliefs* that are shared by the members of an organization, that operate unconsciously, and that define in a basic 'taken-for-granted' fashion an organization's view of itself and its environment" (p. 6). The cultural metaphor can be helpful, but the concept of organizational culture is one borrowed from the corporate world and can also cause problems. The concept is similar to that of a community, but it is not the same. All schools may have cultures, but not all schools are communities. The idea of a school as a learning community suggests a kind of connectedness among members that resembles what is found in a family, a neighborhood, or some other closely knit group, where bonds tend to be familial or even sacred. Such connections may exist in a few corporations; by and large, however, the bonds are likely to be more calculated and instrumental than in a school functioning as a community.

Factors of size and purpose make it difficult to apply concepts of organizational culture, as understood in the corporate world, to schools. As Robert J. Starratt (1990) points out, schools "for the most part. . . [are] too small to suit the powerful abstractions employed in managerial or organizational talk. Such talk is similarly inappropriate, for example, for a family unit. One does not talk of the chief executive officer of a family; neither does one worry about problems of span of control, or indeed of productivity. Such terminology sounds pretentious in a familial setting. Schools are much closer to families than to large corporations, not only in size, but in affect and in focus" (p. 3).

How should schools be understood as learning communities? Communities are defined by their centers — repositories of values, sentiments, and beliefs that provide the needed cement for bonding people together in a common cause (Shils, 1961). Centers govern what is valuable to a community. They provide norms that guide behavior and give meaning to community life. Community centers operate much as official religions do, providing norms that structure what we do, how we do it, and why we do it. The norms become compass settings or sometimes maps that guide our journey through community life. They answer questions: What is this school about? What is our image of learners? What makes us unique? How do we work

together as colleagues? How does this school, as a community, fit
into the larger school community? How do parents fit in? In
schools, community norms are tempered by the professional
norms that define what it is to be a teacher and commit us to the
professional ideal.

How do community norms work? Over the years, Garfield
School, in Milwaukee, Wisconsin, had a reputation for being a
troubled school — that is, until a new principal, Tom McGinnity,
and a dedicated band of Garfield teachers decided to do something about it. As one school board member, cited in an article
by Mary Van de Kamp Nohl (1989) described the situation,
Garfield had "some real hard-core bad teachers, the worst the
district had to offer." According to Van de Kamp Nohl "Garfield
School had the three R's all right: rotten students, reject teachers
and a renegade principal. They were hardly the ingredients to
transform the city's worst school into a national model. But they
did" (p. 72).

How did they do it? Principal McGinnity and some of his
staff worked to create a community within Garfield. As progress
was made, a system of norms emerged, which became a powerful
influence.

> In the new Garfield peer pressure was a powerful
> self-policing force. Accounts of teachers who didn't
> carry their weight — and that meant more than the
> minimum outlined in the contract — traveled
> through the grapevine. . . . Other teachers, inten-
> tionally or not, began to apply the screws — the cold
> shoulder, disapproving glances, curt remarks. They
> complained constantly to Mr. McGinnity about this
> teacher and another who seemed bent on coasting
> to retirement, hoping he could get rid of them. . . .
> Instead, Mr. McGinnity became intensely inter-
> ested in those teachers' work. He was always pop-
> ping into their classrooms, offering hints and sug-
> gesting strategies, reinforcing anything positive.
> He sent them to special courses. If he couldn't
> reform them, perhaps he thought he might make

them uncomfortable enough to leave. Eventually,
one retired, and the other took an extended sick
leave [Van de Kamp Nohl, p. 76].

In the case of Garfield, the norm system focused attention
on school problems that had been invisible. When norms are
violated, problems surface and become legitimate topics of
discussion. Once problems are legitimate, they lend themselves
to resolution. Without such norms, problems remain hidden—
indeed, unofficial, often beyond resolution. Teachers at Garfield
became concerned not only with their own practice but with the
overall practice of teaching at Garfield. Had this not happened,
McGinnity would not have been able to resolve the problems he
faced. He did not expect teachers to conform to his notions or
views, but rather to the norms, which began to define the school
as a community. Relying on norms greatly increases the chances
for success.

Yvonne Davis, former principal of Griffin Elementary
School, Los Angeles, describes her efforts to transform the
school into a community:

The staff was diversified, as most staffs are, with
emergency-credentialed teachers to teachers with
twenty years' experience, with bilingual Spanish-
and Cantonese-speaking teachers to monolingual
teachers, with didactic-style teachers to hands-
on–style teachers, and with teachers who stayed
close to the teacher's desk to teachers who gave a
high degree of attention and close contact to students. These diversities did not change abruptly,
nor did they need to. Rather, things seemed to
"relax"; teachers were more open to trying out new
techniques, new styles, new activities. There was
more respect for each other's efforts, regardless of
style, years of experience, or language of the program. There was a great sense of sharing. Talk in the
lunchroom was dominated by sharing of new ideas
or inquiries about each other's programs. We went

from each teacher's doing his or her own thing to
teachers' sharing ideas and knowing what was
going on in others' rooms and throughout the different grade levels. Working together by grade levels, teachers identified pivotal concepts and skills
and shared ideas on how best to teach them. Teachers felt a strong sense of accountability for students'
success. Eventually, the total school's academic
strengths and weaknesses were analyzed. It was no
longer a voice concerned only for "my class" or "my
kids." Instead, all efforts and energies joined force
to improve the school as a whole.

As the school became more and more a community, the
practice of teaching at Griffin was transformed from an individual to a collective one. As a collective practice becomes
established in a school, the principal can afford to give much
less attention to the traditional management functions of planning, organizing, controlling, and leading, for these become
built in to the everyday life of the school. As Davis explains, "My
role became one of 'acknowledger.' I recognized and acclaimed
good teaching, positive student results, caring parents, and
progress toward our goal at every available opportunity. As
people felt more appreciated, I think they worked harder and
felt more confident to try out and share new ideas. At that point,
my role became one of 'supporter,' 'reinforcer,' and 'facilitator.'"

Since teachers inevitably become key members of the
school as a learning community, they have a special obligation to
help construct the center of shared values. This center in turn
spells out certain morally held duties, responsibilities, and obligations of teachers. Among these is the commitment to do one's
best to make the community work and work well. In practical
language, this means that teachers work diligently, practice in
exemplary ways, keep abreast of new ideas, help other members
of the learning community be successful, and do whatever else is
necessary for the community to function and flourish.

Ann Leonard, a principal in Cooperopolis, California,
sums up her approach to leadership as follows: "Use shared

leadership, with a heavy emphasis on following a vision rather than a person." She works hard at creating and maintaining shared values as a basis for community building in her school, and she works hard at linking what is done in the school to this community core. Initially, Leonard worried that community building was taking precious time from her management and supervisory responsibilities. She sees things differently now:

> I've watched a metamorphosis occur at the school. Those less-than-committed staff members, who I thought needed closer supervision than I could manage, are now working harder and putting in more work hours because of a shared vision we have developed together. . . . The staff is not working harder and longer hours because I'm a charismatic leader, or because I'm using a carrot to reward or a stick to punish. These people are working toward realizing a goal that they believe in, and their internal motivation takes much of the burden of motivation and management off me. That gives me more time to devote to finding the resources we need to have in order to realize our dreams.

A key question is whether the norms and core values that comprise the community center will continue to act as substitutes for leadership even after the leader leaves. Irwin Blumer, a superintendent in Newton, Massachusetts, thinks so. When he was an administrator in the Concord and Concord–Carlisle School District (Massachusetts), he worked for the values of respect for human differences and commitment to full integration of minority students into the ongoing life of the school. He used those values as a basis for guiding everything that was done in the school. Reflecting on his experience, he says:

> One always wonders whether a core value has really become deeply embedded in a school system or whether it is simply something staff and others respect as long as "the leader" is there to push it.

Perhaps the most satisfying moment for me came when I left the school district to become superintendent in another community. The individual who replaced me is a very competent administrator with superb leadership skills. I've been away from the district now for one and one-half years and am pleased to report that the commitment of the school district is as strong and as compelling as when I was present. While it has taken different forms and different shapes under the new superintendent of schools, the commitment to the value remains.

Core values are not set in stone, nor are they easily changed. They are resilient enough to withstand casual change yet flexible enough to accommodate new imperatives that may arise.

The Professional Ideal as a Substitute for Leadership

When we think of professionalizing teaching, our attention is typically drawn to issues of competence, such as toughening standards and improving preparation programs. There are, however, two sides to the ledger of professionalism: competence and virtue. Enhancing the competence side is admittedly a long-term proposition, but school leaders can do much to enhance the virtue side while working in the broader context to improve competence. Enhancing the virtue side means establishing a moral basis for practice.

According to Weick and McDaniel (1989), the more substitutes for leadership, the more likely it is that schools will approximate professional organizations. They point out that substitutes for leadership account for much of what exists in professional organizations, and they cite Kerr (1977) as follows:

There are several reasons why the working environment of professionals employed in organizations presents special opportunities for leadership substitutes to flourish and hierarchical leadership to be consequently less important. The professional's

> expertise, normally acquired as a result of spe-
> cialized training in a body of abstract knowledge,
> often serves to reduce the need for structuring
> information; furthermore, a belief in peer review
> and collegial maintenance of standards often
> causes the professional to look to fellow profes-
> sionals rather than to the hierarchical leader for
> what informational needs remain [Weick and
> McDaniel, p. 343].

Alasdair MacIntyre (1981) defines professional values as
the virtues that enable one to practice in an exemplary way, and
which result in the accomplishment of valued social ends. Albert
Flores (1988) adds to this dimension the ability "to engage in a
practice informed by the virtues. . . [in a fashion that] contributes as well to strengthening and enhancing the growth and
development of a practice. This is because the exercise of the
virtues uniquely defines our relationship with all those other
practitioners with whom we share the same purposes, goals, and
standards of excellence, such that the singular realization of
these internal goods naturally contributes to the overall flourish-
ing of a practice" (p. 7). Taken together, these components
comprise the professional ideal.

Commitment to exemplary practice means practicing at
the edge of teaching, by staying abreast of new developments,
researching one's practice, trying out new approaches, and so
on. In a sense, it means accepting responsibility for one's own
professional development. Moving toward "valued social ends"
means placing oneself in service to students and parents and to
the school and its purposes. The heart of professionalism in
teaching may be a commitment to the caring ethic. The caring
ethic requires far more than bringing state-of-the-art technical
knowledge to bear on one's practice; this results too often in
students' being treated antiseptically, as clients or cases. The
caring ethic means doing everything possible to serve the learning, developmental, and social needs of students as persons.

Concern for the practice of teaching itself is key to the
professional ideal. For example, there is an important difference

between being concerned with one's teaching practice and being concerned with the practice of teaching. The latter concern is directed not only to the broad issues of teaching knowledge, policy, and practice but also to the practical problems and issues that teachers face every day in their classrooms and schools. As the professional ideal becomes established in a school, it is no longer acceptable for one person to teach competently in the company of others who are having difficulty, without offering help. It is not enough to have special insights into teaching but not share them with others. It is not enough to define success in terms of what happens in one's own classroom when the school itself may be failing. It is a question of "one for all, and all for one."

When the professional ideal does get attention, the focus is typically on the development of ethical rules designed to govern teachers' behavior. Rules are concerned with how teachers relate to students and parents, on the assumption that students and their parents depend on teachers' expertise and are vulnerable to teachers' authority. Expertise and position are forms of power, which can be used by teachers and administrators to dominate, exploit, or otherwise take advantage of people with less power. Flores (1988, p. 7) says that students and parents "have little choice but to invest their relationship with trust. . . . To assume that this investment is warranted, professionals are expected to refrain from acts that would violate a client's trust." For these reasons, it is important to begin a serious conversation about developing codes of ethics that define the duties and moral responsibilities of teachers.

In the absence of such a code at the national level, school leaders should work with teachers and teachers' associations to establish local codes. Such codes should be concerned with relationships to students and parents and should also include the regulation of conduct in such areas as relationships with colleagues and provision of good service. Codes can provide the basis for self-regulation and can help build confidence in teachers and sustain teachers' integrity in the eyes of the public.

Professional codes of ethics are helpful and necessary, but they are not enough. Conforming to a code, without making a commitment to its ideals and values, means giving only the appearance of ethical behavior. As Flores (1988, p. 2) explains, "It is important to note that acting ethically and being ethical are substantially different. One can do the right thing, but for the wrong reasons, as, for example, when a person is honest as a way of manipulating another. We would not regard such a person as a morally good person. It is this distinction that is obscured by restricting professionalism to the adherence of the rules."

A teacher may comply with a code requiring parental involvement, not because of her commitment to parents as partners or to democratic values or other ideals, but because she wants to win the parents over and make her life easier. Only when code-specific behavior and underlying ideals and values are connected — only when it is accepted that what teachers do and why they do it are connected — will professional codes cease to be rules of professional etiquette and become powerful moral statements.

Professionalism as virtue is also concerned with questions of character. Commitment to exemplary practice and valued social ends requires one's practice to be linked to the professional's quest for a sense of goodness as a person. This quest in turn makes such values as honesty, fairness, and integrity important. The traditions of teaching, from ancient times to the present, are imbued with moral gravity. The teacher committed to professionalism as virtue acts as a trustee, preserving the traditions and transforming them for the modern context. This process of transformation requires critical reflection, as well as what Aristotle called practical wisdom regarding the purposes of one's practice: "For professionals, being virtuous in this sense means being conscious that one's activities always have a significance beyond the immediacy of particular situations" (Flores, 1988, p. 9).

School administrators have a special responsibility to share in the professional ideal of teaching, for whatever else they are, they are teachers first. (Indeed, one hallmark of the established professions is the preservation of one's professional identity, no matter how far one rises in the administrative ranks.)

Once established in a school, the professional ideal, combined with community norms, becomes a powerful substitute for leadership. From the moral perspective, one purpose of leadership is to establish substitutes like norms and ideals as conditions that make leadership no longer needed. In the next chapter, another substitute for leadership is discussed: the potential to experience intrinsic satisfaction in the work itself.

5

Creating a State of Flow at Work

An underlying theme of this book has been that we humans are driven not only by self-interest but also by our emotions, values, and beliefs, and by the social bonds that emerge from our identification with and membership in various groups. It is not that material rewards are unimportant, or that our psychological needs can be ignored; it is only that neither factor is enough to explain fully what drives us, what motivates us. We are, in some respects, willing to trade a bit of self-interest for more noble ends. It has also been argued that the failure of leadership can be linked directly to our obsession with self-interest and to our resulting neglect of emotion and social bonds.

Nevertheless, we would be remiss in focusing only on emotion and social bonds. In Chapter Two, three motivational rules were summarized:

> What gets rewarded gets done.
> What is rewarding gets done.
> What is good gets done.

"What gets rewarded gets done," a rule based primarily on bureaucratic authority, relies heavily on extrinsic gain to get people to do something. This approach is instrumental, in the sense that someone externally gives something, or promises not to take away something, in return for compliance. It is little more than a trade. People are likely to continue participating in this trade as long as they are getting what they want. Otherwise, people seek either to renegotiate the trade or to back out; involvement in work is calculated. The negative but unantici- pated consequences of overemphasizing this rule are summa- rized by W. Edwards Deming: "People are born with intrinsic motivation, dignity, curiosity to learn, joy in learning. The forces of destruction begin with toddlers—a prize for the best Halloween costume, grades in school, gold stars and on up through the university. On the job, people, teams, divisions are ranked—reward for the one at the top, punishments at the bottom. MBO [management by objectives], quotas, incentive pay, business plans, put together separately, division by division, cause further loss, unknown and unknowable" (cited in Senge, 1990b, p. 7). Commenting on Deming's analysis, Senge (1990b, p. 7) points out that "by focusing on performing for someone else's approval, corporations create the very conditions that predestine them to mediocre performance." Senge believes that superior performance depends on individual and organiza- tional learning, and that both are discouraged by the rule that what gets rewarded gets done.

"What is good gets done" is a rule that asks us to respond because of obligations, duties, a sense of righteousness, felt commitments, and other reasons with moral overtones. This is the approach that emerges when community norms are in place in the school, and when people are committed to the profes- sional ideal (both of these substitutes for leadership are dis- cussed in Chapter Four). People respond to work for internal reasons, and not because someone out there is "leading" them.

"What is rewarding gets done" is a rule somewhere in between the other two. People respond to work for intrinsic reasons, finding what they are doing to be personally significant in its own right. The action is in the work itself. Since involve- ment is intrinsic, no one else has to "lead"; no push or pull from the outside is required. This kind of motivation, being psycho- logical in nature, does not necessarily have substantive moral overtones. Nevertheless, it can still be considered moral, in the sense that people should find meaning in their work, whenever possible and to the greatest extent possible. If this premise is accepted, then school leaders have a moral obligation to do whatever they can to arrange the context of work in a fashion that allows teachers and students to be meaningfully involved. Further, if teachers and others find their work rewarding for intrinsic reasons, still another substitute for leadership will be in place in the school.

What Is Rewarding Gets Done

The importance of the work itself as a motivator has only a recent history in psychology. Frederick Herzberg's famous motivation hygiene theory (Herzberg, Mausner, and Snyderman, 1959) was a pioneering effort. In one of the most replicated studies in the history of management, Herzberg and his colleagues were able to identify two fairly independent sets of job factors that seemed to be important to workers.

One set of factors affects whether people are dissatisfied with their jobs. These, the so-called hygiene factors, seem related to poor performance. Research has suggested that if administrators take care of these factors, so that they are no longer sources of dissatisfaction, workers' performance will improve to the level of "a fair day's work for a fair day's pay"; rarely, however, will workers be motivated to go beyond this minimum contract. For this reason, Herzberg coined the term *hygiene factors* to describe this set, suggesting that they can cause trouble if neglected but are not sources of motivation. They are concerned with the conditions of work, not with the work itself. Conditions of work are the source of extrinsic rewards. Herzberg, Mausner, and Snyderman (1959) concluded that extrinsic rewards are not potent enough to motivate people—at least not for very long, and not without a great deal of effort from administrators.

The second set of factors, called *motivators*, seem not to cause dissatisfaction or poor performance if neglected or even absent. As long as the hygiene factors are in place, people seem to do their jobs in a satisfactory way. The motivators, however, seem to motivate people to go beyond the "fair day's work for a fair day's pay" minimum contract. Motivators are concerned with the work itself, rather than with the conditions of work. The work itself is the source of intrinsic motivation (Herzberg, Mausner, and Snyderman, 1959).

When the motivation-hygiene theory has been tested in school settings (Sergiovanni, 1967), what have tended to emerge as the motivators are a sense of achievement, recognition for good work, challenging and interesting work, and a sense of responsibility for one's work. By contrast, pleasant interpersonal relationships on the job, nonstressful and fair supervision, reasonable policies, and an administrative climate that does not hinder are what have tended to emerge as the hygiene factors. This research has led to the idea that if one can arrange jobs so as to accent opportunities for the motivation factors to be experienced, people will become self-motivated.

The motivation-hygiene theory is not without controversy. Many of its critics feel that the specific findings may well have been artifacts of the methods used by the researchers, portraying an oversimplified version of reality. Nevertheless, few dispute the overall conclusion derived from this research tradition: that, for most people, the work itself counts as an important motivator of work commitment, persistence, and performance.

Carrying this theme further, researchers on job enrichment have identified ways in which jobs can be restructured to allow for workers to experience greater intrinsic satisfaction. Perhaps the best-known study is Hackman and Oldham's (1976). These researchers and their colleagues have identified three psychological states believed to be critical in determining whether a person will be motivated at work:

> *Experienced meaningfulness:* "The extent to which a person perceives work as being worthwhile or important, given her or his system of values."
>
> *Experienced responsibility:* "The extent to which a person believes that she or he is personally responsible or accountable for the outcomes of efforts."
>
> *Knowledge of results:* "The extent to which a person is able to determine on a regular basis whether or not the outcomes of her or his efforts are satisfactory" (Hackman, Oldham, Johnson, and Purdy, 1975, p. 57).

When the three psychological states are present, people are likely to feel good, perform well, and continue to perform well, in the effort to experience more of these feelings in the future. When these feelings are experienced, people do not have to depend on someone else to motivate or lead them.

How can school leaders restructure jobs so that the likelihood of experiencing meaningfulness, responsibility, and knowledge of results will be increased? The answer, provided by Hackman and Oldham (1976), is to build in opportunities for teachers to do the following:

- Use more of their talents and skills (skill variety).
- Engage in activities that allow them to see the whole and understand how their contributions fit into the overall purpose or mission (task identity).
- View their work as having a substantial and significant impact on the lives or work of other people (task significance).
- Experience discretion and independence in scheduling work and in deciding classroom arrangements and instructional procedures (autonomy).
- Get firsthand, and from other sources, clear information about the effects of their performance (feedback).

Experiencing Flow at Work

Carrying this work even further, Mihalyi Csikszentmihalyi's research (1990) has led him to conclude that the key to intrinsic motivation is an optimal experience that he calls *flow*, "the state in which people are so involved in an activity that nothing else seems to matter; the experience itself is so enjoyable that people will do it even at great cost, for the sheer sake of doing it" (p. 4).

Searching our own experience, to identify occasions when we have experienced flow, can help us understand the concept. Recall, for example, instances when you were intensely involved in something. Perhaps it was hobby work; hunting or fishing; researching and writing a proposal to change some important aspect of your school; solving a complex problem; giving a talk to the faculty on a topic dear to your heart; teaching a class—an occasion when you were so absorbed in your work and so committed to its outcome that you completely lost track of time. As you worked, you were in total command of your thoughts and actions. It seemed as if you could even anticipate future moves with ease. You knew instinctively how parts fit together and where to get the information you needed. Your concentration was so intense, and everything seemed to be in such harmony, that at the end of this experience your feelings of competence and well-being were enhanced.

Csikszentmihalyi and others who are studying flow believe that it is commonly experienced by people engaged in a wide range of activities, including rock climbing, hunting, surgery, sports playing, rug weaving, long-distance swimming, writing, playing music, and gardening. All that is needed is for the activity to result in a high level of personal enjoyment and satisfaction, on the one hand, and the enhancement of one's feelings of competence and efficacy, on the other. Czikszentmihalyi (1990) believes that there are eight elements that contribute to these feelings:

> First, the experience usually occurs when we confront tasks we have a chance of completing. Second, we must be able to concentrate on what we are doing. Third and fourth, the concentration is usually because the task undertaken has clear goals and provides immediate feedback. Fifth, one acts with a deep but effortless involvement that removes from awareness the worries and frustrations of everyday life. Sixth, enjoyable experiences allow people to exercise a sense of control over their actions. Seventh, concern for the self disappears, yet paradoxically the sense of self emerges stronger after the flow experience is over. Finally, the sense of the duration of time is altered; hours pass by in minutes, and minutes can stretch out to seem like hours. The combination of all these elements causes a sense of deep enjoyment that is so reward-

ing people feel that expending a great deal of energy is worthwhile simply to be able to feel it [p. 49].

To experience flow, one must be convinced that one's skills and insights are strong enough to cope with the challenges at hand. The matching of skills to challenges is critical, for this is a condition of growth. Csikszentmihalyi (1990, p. 74) explains, "In our studies, we found that every flow activity, whether it involved competition, chance, or other dimensions of experience, had this in common: It provided a sense of discovery, a creative feeling of transporting the person into a new reality. It pushed the person to higher levels of performance, and led to previously undreamed-of states of consciousness. In short, it transformed the self by making it more complex. In this growth of the self lies the key to flow activities."

The balance is delicate. Too much challenge in one's job, without the skills necessary for success, can lead to anxiety. Unless skills improve enough to match the challenge, one is likely to withdraw in search of less challenging alternatives. If levels of anxiety are only moderate, one way out is to seek ways in which one's skills can be enhanced. Long-term anxiety, however, can lead to psychological withdrawal from work and to personality disorders.

By the same token, not experiencing enough challenge at work, given one's skills, is likely to lead to boredom. Teachers, for example, can become "deskilled" by having to work narrowly or repetitiously or by using a restricted range of their talents. This condition ultimately takes its toll in loss of commitment and poor performance. When challenge and skills are high enough to matter and are properly balanced, flow can be experienced. Low challenge and skills may lead to a kind of low-level contentment, which can hardly be considered flow, or at least not for long.

The issue of control is also important. Experiencing flow requires one to be in charge of one's own work. But the amount of control wanted is an individual matter, and so a fixed amount of control for everyone can have differential effects. Relationships between challenge and skill seem also to hold for the amount of control wanted, as compared with the amount of control received. Receiving more control than one wants, like having more challenge than skills, results in anxiety, with the same consequences; wanting more control than one receives results in frustration and long-run boredom, with the same consequences. A match between low levels of control wanted and low levels of control received may lead to a kind of short-term contentment but not to flow; the match between moderate to high levels of control wanted and control received are the conditions needed for flow to occur.

Flow can be a powerful substitute for leadership. Sometimes flow just happens as teachers close the classroom door and, on their own, get into the rhythm of their work. But the obstacles are too great for this to happen often enough. In many schools, for example, teaching is heavily scripted by a bureaucratic system that programs what teachers do, when they do it, how they do it, and even why. Few teachers following a script are challenged to work anywhere near their abilities. By the same token, we often give some teachers, particularly new ones, responsibilities for which they are not ready. Teaching jobs are often fragmented and compartmentalized. This makes it difficult for teachers to sense the wholeness of what they are doing. Schedules are beyond their reach. Curricula are mandated from afar. Materials and books are selected by someone else. Teaching is routinized to the point where it becomes habit. And to make it all work, "what gets rewarded gets done" is a rule that is firmly entrenched as the only motivational strategy.

If we want to harness the power of the work itself as a substitute for leadership, then teaching jobs will have to be redesigned, and systems of support will have to be developed in a way that helps teachers work in conditions of job enrichment. Motivation-hygiene theory, job-enrichment theory, and flow theory can help in this effort.

How well is your school doing in relying on the work itself as a substitute for leadership? The inventory shown in Exhibit 5.1 can help you find out. Scores above 50 suggest that the work itself as a substitute for leadership is alive and well in your school, allowing administrators to focus on other things, such as curricula, teaching, parental involvement, and students' welfare. Scores below 34 suggest that much administrative time and effort are being expended on getting teachers to do what they are supposed to. Scores in between may well indicate that although people are doing what they are supposed to do, administrators have to work hard to "motivate them" to go beyond that level.

Intrinsically satisfying work makes sense because it leads to higher levels of commitment and performance. That is the effectiveness side of the equation. Intrinsically satisfying work also makes sense because it is right and good for teachers and others to find their jobs satisfying and meaningful. That is the moral side of the equation.

Exhibit 5.1. The Work Itself as a Substitute for Leadership: Inventory.

	Not at All	Somewhat	Usually	A Great Deal
In my school teaching jobs are structured to allow teachers:				
1. To discover and explore new ideas and possibilities	1	2	3	4
2. To use talents fully and freely	1	2	3	4
3. To experience variety and challenge in their work	1	2	3	4
4. To participate actively and fully in decisions about curriculum and instruction	1	2	3	4
5. To participate actively and fully in decisions about teaching and learning	1	2	3	4
6. To decide their own classroom schedules	1	2	3	4
7. To concentrate for long periods without interruption or interference	1	2	3	4
8. To teach in ways that make sense to them, provided that they meet overall standards	1	2	3	4

**Exhibit 5.1. The Work Itself as a Substitute for Leadership:
Inventory, Cont'd.**

	Not at All	Somewhat	Usually	A Great Deal
In my school, we:				
9. Have a clear sense of what we are about and want to accomplish	1	2	3	4
10. Provide opportunities, outside the official evaluation system, for teachers to get feedback about how well they are doing	1	2	3	4
11. Provide teachers with opportunities to plan and work closely with others, if they so desire	1	2	3	4
12. Encourage teachers to be self-managers	1	2	3	4
13. Emphasize agreement with respect to the broad purposes and values that bond people at work	1	2	3	4
14. Permit teachers to determine their own objectives and outcomes within a framework of purposes and values	1	2	3	4
15. Encourage autonomy and self-determination	1	2	3	4
16. Allow teachers to feel like originators of their own behavior, rather than like pawns manipulated from outside	1	2	3	4
17. Encourage feelings of competence and control and enhanced feelings of efficacy	1	2	3	4

6

Followership First,
Then Leadership

Professionalism and leadership enjoy high standing in the lex-
icon of education. Both are frequently prescribed as cures for
our school problems. But in many ways the two concepts are
antithetical. Beyond a certain point, the more professionalism is
emphasized, the less leadership is needed; the more leadership
is emphasized, the less likely professionalism is to develop. The
point is not to get rid of leadership. Leadership can add a
measure of quality to the most professional of school settings.
But leadership becomes less urgent and less intensive once the
wheels of professionalism begin to turn by themselves. When
this happens, superintendents and principals can spend less
time trying to figure out how to push and pull teachers toward
goals and more time dealing with the broad issues of teaching
and learning, on the one hand, and ensuring financial, moral,
political, and managerial support for the school, on the other.

When conditions are right, professionalism has a way of
encouraging teachers and principals to be self-managers. By the
same token, providing too much leadership discourages professionalism. For example, the principal who insists on being a
strong instructional leader, even though teachers are perfectly
capable of providing all the necessary leadership, forces teachers into dependent roles and removes opportunities and incentives for them to be self-managers. Self-management and professionalism, by contrast, are complementary concepts. One can be
self-managed without being a professional, but one cannot be a
professional without being self-managed.

In Chapter Four, it was suggested that professionalism could be understood as competence plus virtue. *Virtue* was defined as commitment to the professional ideal of exemplary practice in the service of valued social ends and as concern for the practice of teaching itself. The professional ideal, and the norms and values that define the school as a learning community, comprise two powerful substitutes for leadership. When the substitutes are present, teachers and administrators need less leading from the outside; instead, they are moved to action by inner forces — the motivational power of emotion and social bonds.

The relationship between professionalism and self-management can be understood by considering still another dimension of professionalism. The term *professionalism* was derived from the religious setting, where it pertained to the public statement of what one believed and was committed to (Camenisch, 1988). Commitment goes beyond the commitment of those who have made no such "profession"; carried into the modern professions, the concept of professing something, of believing in something, and of bringing an unusual commitment to this idea remains strong and forms the basis of self-management.

One could argue convincingly that while the establishment of the professional ideal in teaching may be a worthy goal, school must still be run somehow until professionalism is fully established. It follows that teachers, principals, parents, and students will still have to be "motivated" and "led" if the work of the school is to be done and done well. But what about the possibility that self-management could be encouraged by school leaders even if the professional ideal were not fully established? I believe that is possible. Professionalism helps, but so does the power of community norms. Schools as learning communities also publicly proclaim what they believe, and this center of shared values can also become the basis of self-management. Moving in this direction, however, means changing our understanding of leadership.

The Old Leadership Recipe

If self-management is our goal, then leadership will have to be reinvented in a fashion that places "followership" first. At the operational level, leadership is about two things: trying to figure out what needs to be done to make the school work and work well, and trying to figure out how to get people to do these things. For most of the last forty years, we were successful in accomplishing these goals, relying on a very simple management recipe:

- State your objectives.
- Decide what needs to be done to achieve these objectives.
- Translate these work requirements into role expectations.
- Communicate these expectations.
- Provide the necessary training.
- Put people to work.
- Monitor the work.
- Make corrections when needed.
- Throughout, practice human relations leadership, to keep morale up.

In a nutshell, the heart of the recipe was the simple management rule "expect and inspect." Anyone who did not comply with the system was punished in a variety of ways.

But things are different today. The standard recipe does not quite work as well as it used to. The times are different, the situations we face are different, and the people are different. The standard management recipe was based on two kinds of authority (see Chapter Three): bureaucratic (the authority of hierarchy, rules and regulations, job specifications, and assignments) and psychological (the authority of rewards that comes from practicing human relations leadership and fulfilling human needs). There is a place for both, but there are also problems with their use, particularly when bureaucratic and psychological authority comprise the overall strategy for how school administrators manage and lead. One problem is that teachers tend to respond to this kind of authority by becoming subordinates.

From Subordinate to Follower

A major theme of *Value-Added Leadership* (Sergiovanni, 1990) is the importance of building followership in the school, as an alternative to subordination. The argument presented in that work is summarized here.

Subordinates do what they are supposed to do, but little else, and what they do is often perfunctory. Subordinates want "marching orders." They want to know exactly what is expected of them and often gladly do it. For subordinates, life can be uncomplicated and even easy. After all, it does not take much talent or effort to be a good subordinate. If you want to be sure that subordinates are doing what they are supposed to do, in the right way, you have to monitor them and watch over them — either directly, through systems of supervision and evaluation, or indirectly, by monitoring lesson plans, collecting growth plans, analyzing test scores, and using other means.

Relying on psychological authority as the major basis of leadership practice breeds a different kind of subordination, one in which commitment to work depends on the satisfactory exchange of work for rewards: when the right rewards are provided, you get committed work in exchange. But the absence of rewards will mean no committed work, as will the wrong rewards. When rewards get used up — that is, when people are bored with them or no longer interested in them — people are no longer willing to give committed work.

It would be unfair to denigrate the importance of subordination. After all, everyone must adhere to certain minimal responsibilities and minimum standards. Moreover, there are always times when schools would be better if we could only get people to be good subordinates. But can bureaucratic and psychologically based leadership inspire and enhance extraordinary commitment and performance? Can they get people to go beyond — to strive for excellence? Can they build from within the kind of self-management that enables people to function fully, in the absence of rewards and without monitoring? I believe that, in the overwhelming majority of cases, the answer is no. If we want sustained and committed performance from teachers, then we must think about a leadership practice that helps teachers transcend subordination — one that cultivates followership.

What characteristics distinguish followers from subordinates? The ability to be self-managed is primary, of course. Robert E. Kelly (1988) says that followers work well without close supervision, assessing what needs to be done when and how, and making necessary decisions on their own. Followers are people committed to purposes, a cause, a vision of what the school is and can become, beliefs about teaching and learning, values and standards to which they adhere, and convictions. Whatever they are committed to, it is some kind of idea system to which they are connected. In other words, followership requires an emotional commitment to a set of ideas. Once in place, an idea structure constitutes the basis of a leadership practice based on professional and moral authority.

Normally, we think of followers as following charismatic people, or people who have persuasive interpersonal skills. This form of leadership is in the tradition of the managerial mystique, wherein leaders' styles and personalities take precedence over what they believe, intend, and say (see Chapter One). The mystique is an important contributor to the failure of leadership. In the extreme, emphasizing personality over ideas leads to the "messiah syndrome," in which emotional attachment to a leader is so blind and so strong that reason falters.

Neither the managerial mystique nor the messiah syndrome can form the basis of the kind of followership needed in schools. Followership emerges when leadership practice is based on compelling ideas. The concept of followership poses a number of paradoxes. It turns out that effective following is really the same as leadership (Kelly, 1988). Leaders and followers alike are attracted to and compelled by ideas, values, and commitments.

When followership and leadership are joined, the traditional hierarchy of the school is upset. It changes from a fixed form, with superintendents and principals at the top and teachers and students at the bottom, to one that is in flux. The only constant is that neither superintendents and principals nor teachers and students are at the apex; that position is reserved for the ideas, values, and commitments at the heart of followership. Further, a transformation takes place, and emphasis shifts from bureaucratic, psychological, and technical-rational

authority to professional and moral authority. As a result, hierarchical position and personality are not enough to earn one
the mantle of leader. Instead, it comes through one's demonstrated devotion and success as a follower. The true leader is the
one who follows first.

Leadership Through Purposing

Principals and superintendents have special leadership responsibilities. It is up to them to establish followership as the basis of
leadership in the school. One of the ways they do this is to
practice *purposing*. Although it was long considered an imperative of administration, purposing fell in importance as the
managerial mystique strengthened. Today, there is renewed respect for the power of purposing, not only in enhancing the
performance and productivity of people and organizations but
also in providing both with sense and meaning.

Chester Barnard ([1938] 1958) pointed out that purposes
serve as the basis of developing a cooperative system; for Barnard, "the inculcation of belief in the real existence of a common
purpose is an essential executive function" (p. 87). Selznick
(1957) differentiates between the role of the institutional leader
(or what is referred to here as a *community leader*) and that of the
interpersonal leader. In Selznick's words, "the latter's task is to
smooth the path of human interaction, ease communication,
evoke personal devotion, and allay anxiety. His expertness has
relatively little to do with content; he is more concerned with
persons than with policies. His main contribution is to the
efficiency of the enterprise. The institutional leader, on the
other hand, is primarily an expert in the promotion and protection of values" (pp. 27–28). Selznick proposes that the definition
of mission and role and the embodiment of purpose are the two
essential functions of the institutional leader.

Through purposing, school administrators can bring to
the center of their leadership the kind of content and substance
that can help restore meaning to what schools do. As Connie
Goldham, a superintendent in Gorham, Maine, explains, "Today's challenges require us to find some common ground, some

means of collaborative decision making. True change involves looking at what we are doing from a vantage point other than [that of] doing something because that's what teachers (or students or principals or board members) want. We must be able to give reasons for what we do, not only to others but to ourselves. And we must be able to see the connection between why we do what we do and some larger purpose. If we can't see the connection, then maybe we're doing the wrong thing."

Peter Vaill (1984) deserves much of the credit for reviving interest in the concept of purposing, linking it to making enterprises more efficient in the organizational sense, and helping members find meaning and significance in their lives and a sense of community. For Vaill, the term *purposing* refers to "that continuous stream of actions by an organization's formal leadership which has the effect of inducing clarity, consensus and commitment regarding the organization's basic purposes" (p. 57).

Purposing involves both the vision of school leaders and the covenant that the school shares. The notion of vision is widely accepted, but the effect of purposing falls short if this is where it ends. A covenant provides the added dimension of values and moral authority, to make purposing count.

In successful schools, consensus runs deep. It is not enough to have worked out what people stand for and what is to be accomplished; a binding and solemn agreement must emerge, one that represents a value system for living together and forms the basis of decisions and actions. This agreement is the school's covenant. When both the value of vision and the value-added dimension of the covenant are present, teachers and students respond with increased motivation and commitment, and their performance is well beyond the ordinary.

Max de Pree (1989, p. 12) distinguishes between the run-of-the-mill "fair day's work for fair day's pay" contract and a covenant: "Contracts are a small part of a relationship. A complete relationship needs a covenant. . . . A covenantal relationship rests on a shared commitment to ideas, to issues, to values, to goals. . . . Covenantal relationships reflect unity and grace and poise. They are expressions of the sacred nature of the relationships." (The concept of the covenant will be discussed in more detail in Chapter Eight.)

The Practice of Purposing

Newton schools superintendent Irwin Blumer (1989) describes the practice of leadership through purposing:

> *Say it.* Define the core values. Communicate them clearly and often to inside and outside constituencies.
>
> *Model it.* Act on these core values. When it comes time to make tough choices and trade-offs, make it clear that the core values drive the final decisions.
>
> *Organize for it.* Put in resources to support the core values. Organize incentives and rewards for organizational units and personnel whose actions exemplify a commitment to core values. Ensure that the core values permeate all the arenas in the school systems. . . classroom routines, cafeteria, playground, faculty meetings, reward systems, student council, traditions and ceremonies, grouping practices, posters and slogans, curriculum, models of teaching and lesson structures, and spontaneous personal contact.
>
> *Support it.* Provide additional resources to the areas that promote core values. When undergoing retrenchment, cut other areas before jeopardizing programs and practices that reflect the core values. The most important things get cut last.
>
> *Enforce it and commend practices that exemplify core values.* Embody core values in personnel evaluations.
>
> *Express outrage when practices violate the core values.* Outrage is a powerful form of communication. Outrage tells people what is important [pp. 8–9].

The practice of leadership by outrage is discussed in Chapter Nine.

Deal and Peterson (1990) offer many suggestions for the practice of purposing, and they illustrate their suggestions with case studies. In one case, Hank Cotton arrived as the new principal of Cherry Creek High School, in Englewood, Colorado, after five other principals had served within a span of six years. Cherry Creek had once been an excellent school, its reputation based on academic excellence and innovative schooling. By the 1970s, however, the school was having problems with course proliferation, flexible and often unintelligible academic requirements, and student attendance:

> Class attendance [had] declined — to below 80 percent during some class periods. "Teachers" canceled classes when they wished. Sanctions for cutting class and school were not regularly enforced. Over time, the community became increasingly concerned about academic achievement and student drug use. A new superintendent arrived and decided to make some changes. . . . The new superintendent gave Cotton a mandate to make changes and remove some . . . prior innovations.
>
> While it may have been clear to some that problems existed, it was not clear to others. Some parents, students, and faculty were content with how things were. Cotton faced both opportunities for and obstacles to making fundamental changes in the culture of the school. Overcoming the obstacles meant generating conflict and resistance.
>
> He decided to begin by focusing on the importance of student responsibility and academic performance. Cotton believed that attendance was a prerequisite [of] student achievement. He believed that to achieve their potential, students ought to attend class, and that something of value went on in every classroom every day.
>
> Consequently, to deal with prevailing absen-

teeism, he instituted new student attendance policies. The school maintained its open campus—
reiterating the belief that students should learn
adult responsibilities through self-regulation. However, when classes met, students and teachers were
expected to attend.

Some 235 students were soon suspended because of infractions of the policy. Needless to say,
the parents complained, and Cotton was often on
the telephone, explaining the new policy to upset
parents. The policy, however, was easy to relate to
the existing parental values, since students had to
be in class to learn. Student absenteeism dropped
dramatically after the first semester.

Cotton created other new rules. He instituted a new parking policy to keep students' cars
from damaging the school's lawns. As luck would
have it, one of the first cars in violation belonged to
a board member's son. When asked whether it
should be towed, Cotton responded, "Definitely!"
The policy was upheld then and thereafter, no matter who the offender.

At times Cotton even alienated himself from
district colleagues by taking strong, vocal stands on
issues. For example, one year he banned smoking
in the school. No one, not students, teachers, or
administrators, was allowed to smoke on the prem-
ises under threat of suspension or administrative
reprimand. Stress increased. No other school in the
district took the same stand. During one meeting
with the superintendent, Cotton was asked, "Do you
have to do [these things] so flamboyantly?" Cotton's
response was "Wait for the results!"

During many of the confrontations Cotton
had to press ahead alone. Even when some faculty,
parents, or students believed he was right, they
often were unwilling to publicly support his decisions or views. Public support developed slowly.

Cotton's support was based mainly in the changes that helped achieve academically, socially, or athletically valued ends, primarily those that directly supported teachers and their work. For example, Cotton did away with such teacher "administrivia" as responsibilities for signing out textbooks, hall duty, cafeteria duty, study hall supervision, and writing and checking permission passes. Others took on these responsibilities — despised by the teachers — so that teachers could concentrate on teaching. Cotton hoped to build support while reinforcing the belief that teaching, not managing students' routine behavior, was the most important activity of the school.

Teachers value student academic performance. Research indicates it is the most important intrinsic reward they seek. Therefore, one of Cotton's activities during his early years at the school was not to impose new values but to reinforce the existing value teachers and the community placed on student achievement. He raised its relative priority compared to the school's prior emphasis upon equality and noncompetitiveness.

By the 1980s attendance at school and in class became one of the highest in the district, even though students were allowed, when they had [no] scheduled class[es], to leave school grounds at will. They could go to study hall, study in the halls, or simply hang out across the street. While an administrative apparatus was put in place to "catch" offenders, attendance in class came to occur largely because it was part of the school's mores, not because of the fear of sanctions.

The principal helped embed his priorities in the school by practicing what he preached. He modeled his values. While he espoused high standards of performance and professionalism, he also made a point [of] attend[ing] seminars, institutes, and executive development programs to improve his own work. Cotton regularly carried novels or histories around with him, and he quoted from them in his memos. He wrote clearly. He made [it] a point to select other administrators and teachers who were also well read and articulate. He spoke of the value of the world of the intellect and set an example of it.

Cotton reinforced norms of performance and success by recounting stories of the school's achievements. Stories communicate what is important in a simple and direct way. They can help bind faculty to the school by making them feel part of a successful, lively, interesting, and select organization. The history of the school is shared in this oral tradition and expressed by teachers as well as [by] the principal. Cotton was a veritable library of stories of the success of individuals who exemplified the values and traditions of Cherry Creek High School. In talking with outsiders, newcomers, or media people he would start the conversation with . . . stories of successes at the school.

Cotton told a core of a dozen stories. Their basic themes were (1) the importance of innovation; (2) the need for hard, continuous work to achieve success; (3) the ways that quiet students or teachers finally achieve success through continuous struggle; (4) the ways teachers work together to improve classes and enjoy each others' company; (5) the importance of recruiting and selecting only the best teachers available; (6) the importance of varied, quality cocurricular activities to provide choices that meet the needs of students; and (7) the ability of teachers to make a difference in the lives of students. The stories Cotton told covered the range of values, beliefs, and assumptions that expressed the values undergirding the emerging culture.

Cotton made extensive use of ceremonies, rituals, traditions, and symbols to reinforce the new priorities. At Cotton's first graduation at Cherry Creek, students threw cans, tossed paper airplanes, and were generally inattentive. Cotton told the seniors the next year that the graduation ceremony was a problem, and that it needed to be revamped. He involved them in reshaping graduation to elevate its importance. Students now wear caps and gowns in a more formal atmosphere. The ceremony became a valued occasion for students and parents.

Cotton gradually increased the number of ceremonies that celebrated academic and cocurricular success. These ceremonies were made more formal [and] structured and were carefully orchestrated to denote the importance of the event. While he routinely dressed in a coat and tie, Cotton deliberately changed his "uniform" for these ceremonies. He brought a dark suit to school to change into for honors assemblies or evening award ceremonies.

Hank Cotton took over a school that had extensive problems but also had customarily valued educational achievement. By reaffirming this old value and steering the school in some new directions, the principal, over time, reshaped the culture. He focused the school on norms of professionalism, performance, improvement, and collegiality.

The school now recognizes and rewards academic excellence and superior performance in such areas as debate, the school newspaper, and the yearbook. . . . The congruence of school values with community values has [now] been reestablished. The faculty, community, and students share enormous pride in the school and loyalty to its principal [Deal and Peterson, 1990, pp. 37–45].

Purposing and the Stages of Leadership

One way to understand Hank Cotton's approach to leadership is
to view it developmentally, as involving four stages. These stages
are by no means rigid and discrete, but they do provide a pattern
for organizing our thoughts. During each of the stages, Cotton
made clear his own beliefs and convictions regarding schooling.
For example, he believed that for Cherry Creek to succeed, it
had to recapture its time-honored sense of what its values were
as a school. Having made his intentions clear, he practiced
leadership by bartering.

During this stage, leader and led strike a bargain whereby
the leader gives to those led something that they want, in exchange for something the leader wants. The substance of the
bargain may involve exchanging rewards or punishments for
compliance or noncompliance.

In this case, Cotton tightened the system by providing
structures, redefining policies, and strictly enforcing them. Bureaucratic authority was clearly the basis of his leadership practice. His stance was moral, to be sure, but at this stage he did not
appeal so much to what was right and good as to what would and
would not be done. He traded rewards for compliance. Noncompliance brought forth his wrath.

Leadership by bartering helps get things moving when
the goals and interests of the leader and those of the followers
are not the same. Until the goals become similar enough, there is
little or no basis for practicing other forms of leadership. Leadership by bartering is a concept similar to transactional leadership as proposed by James MacGregor Burns (1978).

Once basic compliance was achieved at Cherry Creek,
teachers were able to help shape the new system and share
responsibility for its success. To help matters along, Cotton
practiced leadership through building. He focused his attention
on providing the kind of climate and interpersonal support that
enhanced opportunities for fulfilling the needs for achievement, responsibility, competence, and esteem.

As the faculty began to respond to this sort of leadership,
and as the goals and interests of teachers and principal began to

move closer together, Cotton's leadership was directed to developing shared values and commitments that bound the faculty to a common cause. Leadership through bonding allows the use of moral authority as a basis of leadership. (Leadership through bonding is a concept similar to Burns's transformational leadership.)

Once values and commitments were shared, Cotton was able to step more to the sidelines, practicing leadership through binding. He directed his attention to "tying the bonds together" by institutionalizing improvement gains into the everyday life of the school, concentrating on providing support, and otherwise serving the school's shared values. (The stages of leadership are summarized in Table 6.1.)

Hank Cotton was able to develop and use community norms as a basis of his leadership practice because he understood how leadership strategy and leadership purpose are linked. The failure of leadership has resulted in part from the effort to develop and implement strategies in the absence of purposes. Only when strategies evolve from purposes, however, do they become powerful substitutes for leadership, enabling people to be driven from the inside. The link between leadership purposes and leadership strategies can be illustrated in the following way:

Leadership Purposes ⟶	*Leadership Strategies*
Values	Goals
Norms	Policies
Visions	Forecasts
Directions	Objectives
Frameworks	Blueprints

Relying solely on leadership strategies, without giving thought to purposing, puts people in the position of having to follow someone else's script. This forces them to be subordinates rather than followers.

Balancing Style and Substance

What about the leader's personality or leadership style? Can leadership through ideas really work? Can we rely on persua-

Table 6.1. The Stages of Leadership and School Improvement.

Leadership Stages	Sources of Authority	Leadership Concepts	Involvement of Followers	Needs Satisfied	Effects
Leadership as "Bartering"	Bureaucratic: reliance on rules, regulations, structures, and mandates	Management skills Leadership style Contingency theory Exchange theory Path-goal theory	Calculated	Physical Security Social Ego	Continual performance contingent upon parties keeping the bargain struck: "A fair day's work for a fair day's pay."
Leadership as "Building"	Psychological: reliance on human relations and interpersonal skill	Empowerment Symbolic leadership Charisma	Intrinsic	Esteem Competence Autonomy Self-actualization	Performance and commitment are sustained beyond external conditions. Both are beyond expectations in quantity and quality.

Leadership as "Bonding"	Arousing awareness and consciousness that elevate organizational goals and purposes to the level of a shared covenant and bonds together leader and followers in a moral commitment.	Professional and moral: reliance on common socialization, professional values, felt obligations, and duties	Cultural leadership Moral leadership Covenant	Moral	Purpose Meaning Significance
Leadership as "Binding"	Turning improvements into routines, so that they become second-nature, allowing full attention to new challenges, new improvements.	Moral: reliance on felt obligations and duties	Institutional leadership Servant stewardship	Automatic (as long as things work, people work)	All needs are supported

Performance sustained

Exhibit 3-1 from *Value-Added Leadership: How to Get Extraordinary Performance in Schools* by Thomas J. Sergiovanni, copyright ©1990 by Harcourt Brace Jovanovich, Inc., reprinted by permission of the publisher.

sion, based on the credibility of our arguments? Or must we ultimately resort to personality, cleverness, and the right leadership moves? In the tug-of-war between substance and style, style too often wins.

A victory for style implies an underlying assumption of our leadership practice: that teachers are cast in one mold, school leaders in another. School leaders can respond to what is good, right, and sensible; apparently, teachers cannot, and so leaders must resort to clever psychological techniques to get teachers to respond.

The evidence indicates otherwise, however. Teachers are just as capable of responding to what is good, right, and sensible as school leaders are. All it takes is for school leaders to practice at the midpoint in this tug-of-war: use enough "style" to build an interpersonal climate characterized by trust, and demonstrate enough knowledge of and commitment to issues of substance to build integrity.

Donald D. Gainey, principal of Rhode Island's West Warwich High School, found that midpoint: "I wanted to assist teachers in opening a dialogue about their craft, to observe many of their students in different settings, to build a more global vision of the mission of the school from different perspectives, and to break through the isolated feeling of high school teachers." To achieve this goal, Gainey introduced two new programs to West Warwich High School: a peer coaching program, and the Together Everyone Achieves More (TEAM) program. The initial reaction of the faculty was reluctance to participate. Teachers feared that they might have to get involved in evaluating their peers. Gainey decided to push ahead anyway and developed workshops designed to acquaint teachers with what peer coaching was and how it worked. Using himself as a model, he frequently served as the "teacher" to be observed and coached. One aim of the workshops was to stress the reflective, nonthreatening, nonjudgmental, and nondirective nature of the process of peer coaching and conferencing. Because Gainey put himself on the firing line, so to speak, these themes became rich with validity. As a result, a number of teachers decided to give the program a try. As the program became established, others opted to join in. Gainey explains:

> Initially, these programs were not greeted with open arms by the teachers. The average tenure of the faculty is twenty years of service. Nevertheless, they are cautiously open to new ideas, if they can see the potential benefits for themselves and students. My basic approach was first to convince the teachers to go through the training and give the program a try. I was able to achieve this by convincing them that the worst possible scenario would be that they might learn some new strategies to add to their repertoire. Once they were hooked, I asked a faculty member to coordinate the program and to consult with me about the administrative details only. The confidentiality of who was observing whom and what the outcomes of these observations were was maintained. The best part of these programs is that, after my initial involvement, the teachers' successes were based on their efforts. They did it themselves.

Motivational technology, change theory, and the skilled application of leadership styles certainly all contribute to the success of ventures like this one. Ultimately, however, it is not just personality that counts. At least equally important is the leader's ability to establish a climate of trust and a sense of integrity in the ideas being proposed. Key to this effort is something worth following. Without ideas, values, and commitments, there can be no followership. Without followership, there can be no leadership. In this sense, the most basic principle of leadership is "followership first, then leadership."

7

Collegiality as a Professional Virtue

There is widespread agreement that collegiality among teachers is an important ingredient of promoting better working conditions, improving teaching practice, and getting better results. Susan J. Rosenholtz (1989) has found collegiality to be an important element that differentiates "learning enriched" from "learning impoverished" schools. Roland Barth (1990), perhaps the most compelling voice for collegiality, views it as key to his conception of the school as a community of learners.

But collegiality has benefits beyond improving the workplace and contributing to learning. Understood as a form of professional virtue, collegiality is another powerful substitute for leadership. The more this virtue becomes established in a school, the more natural connections among people become, and the more they become self-managed and self-led, so that direct leadership from the principal becomes less necessary. Despite its importance, true collegiality is rare in schools.

Johnson (1990) describes the situation in this way:

> In the ideal world of schooling, teachers would be true colleagues working together, debating about goals and purposes, coordinating lessons, observing and critiquing each other's work, sharing successes and offering solace, with the triumphs of their collective efforts far exceeding the summed accomplishments of their solitary struggles. The real world of schools is usually depicted very differ-

86

ently, with teachers sequestered in classrooms, encountering peers only on entering or leaving the building. Engaged in parallel piecework, they devise curricula on their own, ignoring the plans and practices of their counterparts in other classrooms or grades; when it occurs, conversation offers a diversion from teaching rather than the occasion for its deliberation—travel plans rather than lesson plans are said to dominate faculty-room talk. Although such portrayals are often exaggerated, they contain more truth that most of us would like to believe [p. 148].

In their biting analysis of the world of teaching, Ann Lieberman and Lynne Miller (1984) conclude, "For most teachers in most schools, teaching is indeed a lonely enterprise. With so many people engaged in so common a mission in so compact a space and time, it is perhaps the greatest irony—and the greatest tragedy of teaching—that so much is carried on in self-imposed and professionally sanctioned isolation" (p. 11). Johnson (1990) concludes that the barriers to achieving collegiality in schools are both structural and attitudinal. They include "poorly designed schedules, inadequate time, random room assignments, or the absence of meaningful subunits within schools, [which] can discourage new collegial ventures and undo existing ones" (p. 178). She believes that these problems can be remedied by school leaders who are serious about the value of collegiality. For example, teachers need sufficient time to meet. The school schedule must be arranged to encourage rather than impede opportunities for teachers to interact. The pace of teaching must be modified, to permit reflection. For Johnson, "very few teachers have more than one hour of unassigned time each day, time already insufficient for all that must be done to prepare lessons, grade papers, and confer with students. Teachers [in her study] routinely said that short-term obligations to their students took precedence over long-term goals of improving their practice or their schools" (p. 172).

In their research, Judith Warren Little (1987) and Susan

Rosenholtz (1989) found that the kind of leadership that principals provided influenced the collegial norm structure of
schools. Rosenholtz found that teachers in high-collegiality
schools described their principals as supportive and as considering problems to be schoolwide concerns that provided opportunities for collective problem solving and learning. Despite the
isolating effects of the structure of schooling and the bureaucratic hindrances of tight schedules, such principals figured out
ways to get around impediments to collegiality. By contrast,
teachers and principals in less collegial schools reported feeling
isolated and alienated. Little (1987) found that norms of collegiality were developed when principals clearly communicated
expectations for teachers to cooperate. The principals offered
themselves as models for collegiality by working directly with
teachers in school improvement and rewarding expressions of
collegiality among teachers. They provided recognition, release
time, money, and other resources, and they protected teachers
who were willing to buck the customary norms of privatism and
isolation by engaging in collegial behaviors.

The School's Culture

Collegiality and school culture are connected. For example,
among the prerequisites that Johnson (1990) identifies for collegiality are good teachers and the right organizational norms.
When collaboration was present, the teachers in Johnson's study
"spoke of 'good' or 'outstanding' teachers as those who are committed and generous, who are open to change and eager to
learn, and who see beyond their own private successes and
failures." As one teacher put it, teachers who collaborate are "not
just good teachers, they're good people" (p. 167).

The culture of most schools is characterized by norms of
privatism and isolation, which keep teachers apart. Furthermore, although administrators often talk about the value of
collegiality, their actions sometimes encourage teachers to compete, rather than cooperate. Moreover, breaking with the norms
of isolation and privatism can make teachers more vulnerable to
censure and criticism from administrators.

Johnson (1990) believes that even if administrators authentically encourage collegiality, teachers themselves must ultimately take responsibility for its establishment. She is convinced that the removal of administrative barriers does not alone ensure that teachers will cooperate: "Strong norms of autonomy and privacy prevail among teachers. Creeping fears of competition, exposure of shortcomings, and discomfiting criticism often discourage open exchange, cooperation, and growth. Until teachers overcome such fears and actively take charge of their own professional relations, teaching will likely remain isolating work. The initiative is theirs, but the responsibility for creating more collegial schools cannot be theirs along" (p. 179).

The problem seems to result partly from a culture of schooling whose management is captured by bureaucratic norms and whose teachers are captured by the norms of isolation and privatism. These norms seem impervious to change strategies and leadership practices that rely on bureaucratic, psychological, and technical-rational authority. Moreover, rules and mandates, heightened practice of human relations, and appeals to what the research says seem relatively unable to affect the normative structure of a school. For example, administrators who push for collegiality by altering structures and introducing such innovations as team teaching and peer coaching in a school, without addressing the norm structure, may be superimposing a form of collegiality on an unaccepting culture. When this is the case, collegial practices are merely grafted onto the existing school culture (Grimmitt, Rostad, and Ford, forthcoming). One has, in other words, a form of contrived collegiality. Hargreaves (1989) describes contrived collegiality as characterized by "formal, specific bureaucratic procedures to increase the attention being given to joint teacher planning and consultation. It can be seen in initiatives such as peer coaching, mentor teaching, joint planning and specially provided rooms, formally scheduled meetings, and clear job descriptions and training programs for those in consultive roles. These sorts of initiatives are administrative contrivances designed to get collegiality going in schools where little has existed before" (p. 6).

Contrived collegiality, by forcing people together, can take a toll
on teachers' time and compromise their professional autonomy.

The receiving culture is key in determining whether ad-
ministratively induced collegiality is contrived or becomes real.
If, as Ann Lieberman (1988) and her colleagues suggest, the
existing culture were transformed into a professional culture
and the school itself were transformed into a learning community, then collegiality would become real. For this transformation to occur, change strategies and leadership practices must
be based primarily on professional and moral authority. In a
sense, it is a problem of getting the "vaccine" right. In this case,
cultural problems require cultural solutions.

From the discussion so far, it appears that Johnson's
(1990) notion of the good teacher and the right culture are
important prerequisites. Without them, efforts to promote collegiality will not result in the real thing. When it is connected to
conceptions of the good teacher and to the right receiving
culture, however, collegiality can become firmly established in
schools as a form of professional virtue.

The Dimensions of Virtue

There are two dimensions of collegiality as professional virtue.
The first involves the fulfillment of obligations that stem from
memberships—in the case of the school, membership in the
teaching profession and in the school as a community. Professional and community memberships provide teachers with certain rights and privileges and exact certain obligations and
duties. One has the right to expect help and support from other
members, and the obligation to give the same; collegiality is
reciprocal, in the same way that friendship is. For teachers
and principals, the obligation of collegiality involves cooper-
ating and giving support for carrying out professional
responsibilities.

The second dimension of collegiality has to do with why
one behaves collegially. As Craig K. Ihara (1988) points out,
"Collegiality must . . . be understood as more than proper *behavior* toward one's colleagues. Collegiality is better defined in

terms of having the proper professional attitude or orientation. To take this approach to collegiality is to consider it a kind of professional virtue" (p. 57). Why behave collegially? Because it is effective to do so, on the one hand, and good to do so, on the other.

Up to this point, the discussion can be summarized as follows. Collegiality cannot be understood in the abstract. What makes two people colleagues is common membership in a community, commitment to a common cause, shared professional values, and a shared professional heritage. Without this common base, there can be no meaningful collegiality.

As Barth (1990) points out, much of what passes in schools as collegiality is really congeniality. Congeniality emerges from the friendly human relationships that exist in a school and is characterized by loyalty, trust, and easy conversation among teachers, factors that often lead to the development of a closely knit social group. When congeniality is high, a strong informal culture aligned with social norms emerges. But these norms may or may not facilitate collegiality. For example, sometimes the norms reinforce the very conditions that make schools ineffective. Congeniality without collegiality is often a by-product of leadership strategies and practices that rely too heavily on psychological authority. Collegiality, by contrast, is connected to the existence of norms and values that define the faculty as a community of like-minded people bonded in common commitment. Because of shared work goals and a common work identity, they feel obligated to work together for the common good.

Congeniality, in the form of interpersonal loyalty and affection, has its merits. Indeed, congeniality, in combination with the professional ideal, contributes to the establishment and nurturance of collegiality, and its absence is not necessary for collegiality to be present. What is necessary is mutual respect. Respect, in this context, means mutual confidence in abilities and intentions: "Respect for a person's expertise entails acting in ways that rely on that knowledge and competence. One who has respect for someone's special knowledge and skills will be confident that he or she will act knowledgeably and skillfully. Respect for a professional's commitment to professional ideals and standards also entails [a] kind of confidence — concerning not the person's capacities, but his or her intentions" (Ihara, 1988, p. 58).

We have now identified several elements of collegiality as virtue: a conception of the good person, who values collegiality for its own sake; connectedness to a community, which entitles one to be treated collegially and obliges one to treat others collegially; and interpersonal relationships characterized by mutual respect.

Collegiality and the Control Paradox

How is collegiality linked to better teaching and to more effective schools? What are the consequences for teachers' performance and school outcomes when collegiality is lacking? How does collegiality work as a substitute for leadership?

These questions can be answered in part through an examination of how the control paradox in management is resolved. Mintzberg (1979) says, "Every organized human activity . . . gives rise to two fundamental and opposing requirements: the *division of labor* into various tasks to be performed and the *coordination* of these tasks to accomplish the activity. The structure of an organization can be captured simply as the sum total of ways in which it divides its labor into distinct tasks and then achieves coordination among them" (p. 2). Every school leader faces the same control problem. How should the work of teaching and learning be divided? Once divided, how should it be coordinated, so that control is maintained and things make sense as a whole? Individual teachers have important things to do, but those things must be done in coordination with what others are doing if schools are to work well. An emphasis on differentiation may make coordination difficult; emphasis on coordination may mean less differentiation.

One way to solve the control paradox is through collegiality as a substitute for leadership. But there are five other strategies as well, and each one has different consequences for the school. The six strategies are (1) directly and closely supervising teachers, (2) standardizing the work of teaching, (3) standardizing the outcomes of teaching, (4) emphasizing professional socialization, (5) emphasizing purposing, and (6) structuring for collegiality and natural interdependence. In a tactical sense, any of the six could be used appropriately at one time or another, but the chosen strategy must be matched to the amount of complexity found in the work itself and in the work environment. Such matching is critical: if the strategy does not fit the level of complexity, the level of complexity will change to match the strategy. This is a variation on the management rule "If form does not follow function, function will be shaped to fit the form." Thus a simple strategy applied to the normally complex work of teaching will simplify the work, with negative effects on what is learned and how it is learned.

The six control strategies are based on a typology proposed by Mintzberg (1979). The typology has been expanded to include the work of Weick (1986) and Peters and Waterman (1982).

Direct Supervision

The simplest way to control the work of people who have different responsibilities is to have one of those people take responsibility for the work of others. The designated leader provided directions, close supervision, and inspection and otherwise executes the well-known planning, organizing, controlling, directing, motivating, and evaluating chain of management functions. This approach works best for simple work done in a routine fashion. Direct supervision may be a highly appropriate control strategy for fast-food restaurants but not for schools, where work is much more complex. Direct supervision is based on bureaucratic authority and is implemented smoothly when accompanied by competent human relations–based leadership.

Standardized Work Processes

Standardized work processes represent a form of coordination achieved on the drawing board before work is actually undertaken (Mintzberg, 1979). This strategy works best in highly determinate and predictable environments. When work processes are standardized, what teachers are to do and how they are to do it is programmed or scripted. One "best" way to do things is assumed. Highly detailed and tightly connected curricula, and teaching and evaluation alignment strategies that comprise instructional delivery systems, are examples of standardized work processes. This strategy may make sense for Federal Express but not for schools, where work is more complex. One key to standardizing work processes is to rely on research and other technical-rational efforts in identifying one "best" way. Human relations–based leadership is also helpful. Bureaucratic authority is present as well, to enforce the management systems that support work standardization.

Standardized Outputs

Standardized outputs as a form of control are achieved when everyone is required to produce similar products or reach the same level of performance. In schools, this goal can be met with standardized tests, measurable objectives, and other standard outcome indicators used in getting people to do what they are supposed to do. Standardizing outputs can be different from standardizing work processes in that once output requirements are set, people can be left free to decide how they are going to meet them. Offering such discretion is a strength of this strategy. An important concern, however, is whether output requirements for schools can be standardized and specified in enough detail for everyone to know what has to be accomplished but not in so much detail that the curriculum is unduly narrowed and needs based on individual differences are ignored. Standardized outputs may ultimately compromise the degree of freedom that people have with respect to work processes. For example, defining good schooling in terms of highly specific levels of gain on standardized tests may well dictate how principals, teachers, and students must spend their time, how teachers must teach, what students must learn, and how they must learn (to the exclusion of other, perhaps more suitable, choices). How outputs are defined determines the different bases of authority for leadership that emerge. When goals are seen as objectives, there is a tilt toward bureaucratic and technical-rational authority. When goals are seen as values, the tilt is toward professional and moral authority.

Professional Socialization

In relying on professional socialization, one need not standardize either work processes or outputs to solve the control paradox. The term *professional socialization* means the upgrading of the knowledge base for teaching and an emphasis on teachers' professional obligations. Once a professional level of training and socialization has been attained, teachers presumably will know what to do, when they ought to do it, and how to do it. They respond on the basis of professional authority.

Professional socialization is the way in which more advanced professions solve the control paradox. As Mintzberg (1979) points out, "When an anesthesiologist and a surgeon meet in the operating room to remove an appendix, they need hardly communicate: by virtue of their respective training, they know exactly what to expect of each other" (p. 7). Professional socialization has a great deal of merit, but it is less a strategy for school leaders than a long-term strategy for upgrading the entire profession. As upgrading occurs, issues of coordination and control will become less difficult to resolve. Like the professional ideal, professional socialization functions as a substitute for leadership and as a substitute for external controls.

Purposing and Shared Values

As a form of control, purposing and shared values can provide the substance of symbol management, furnishing the "glue" that binds people in a loosely connected world. They can also constitute the center around which one constructs the school as a learning community.

Collegiality and Natural Interdependence

When collegiality and natural interdependence are used, the control paradox can be solved through informal communication and the need for people to cooperate in order to be successful. Collegiality concerns the extent to which work values are held in common and the extent to which teachers help one another as a result. Natural interdependence has to do with the extent to which teachers must work together and cooperate in order to get the job done properly. This control strategy relies heavily on professional and moral authority.

Professional socialization, purposing and shared values, and collegiality and natural interdependence are unique in that they can solve the control paradox under loosely structured conditions by providing the kind of normative power needed to get people to meet commitments. They are also unique in that, once in place, they are able to transform teachers from subordinates to self-managers. These strategies are also well matched to the complex behaviors required in successful teaching and learning. Direct supervision may be effective for simple work. As work gets more complex, the emphasis must shift, from direct supervision to standardized work, standardized outputs, and emphasis on professional socialization, purposing, collegiality, and natural interdependence (Mintzberg, 1979). Relationships between control strategies and teaching behavior are shown in Table 7.1.

When professional socialization, purposing and shared values, and collegiality are emphasized, they become substitutes for leadership. This means that direct leadership from administrators can be less intense—indeed, much more informal. Issues of control and coordination take care of themselves naturally as teachers and administrators respond to internalized forces. Simple management systems tend to free people for complex behavior.

By contrast, direct supervision, standardized work, and standardized outputs, understood as objectives rather than values, are simple ideas that typically require complex management systems. Before they can work, structures must be in place and roles must be identified and linked. Furthermore, expectations must be explicit, and systems of monitoring and inspection must ensure that the system is operating properly. Interper-

Table 7.1. Control Strategies and Consequences.

	Direct Supervision	Standardized Work	Standardized Outputs	Professional Socialization	Purposing and Shared Values	Collegiality and Interdependence
Strategy concept	Simple	Simple	Simple	Complex	Complex	Complex
Management system	Complex	Complex	Moderate	Simple	Simple	Simple
Teachers' behavior	Simple	Simple	Moderate	Complex	Complex	Complex
Authority for leadership	Bureaucratic, psychological	Technical-rational, bureaucratic, psychological	Typically technical-rational, psychological	Professional	Moral	Professional, moral
Management values emphasized	Secular authority, science, deductive logic			Sense experience, intuition, sacred authority, emotion		

sonal leadership must also be constant and intense, if the system is to work. As the management system becomes increasingly complex, the discretion of teachers is narrowed. Their behavior becomes more scripted. As a result, teaching becomes more simple.

In short, complex structures result in simple behaviors, and simple structures result in complex behaviors. Moreover, simple ideas require complex systems for implementation, and complex ideas require simple systems.

Despite the problems, direct supervision, standardized work, and standardized outputs remain popular because they reflect the official values of management. Because the management values undergirding professional socialization, shared values, and collegiality remain largely unofficial, the widespread use of these control strategies is hindered.

What is the connection between collegiality and leadership? As the norm of collegiality becomes established, leadership increasingly takes care of itself. It becomes part of the everyday expression of teachers and principals at work. Teachers depend more on their own wits and on their colleagues, and the pressure on administrators is eased. Administrators in turn worry less about providing direct interpersonal leadership and put more effort into establishing the conditions that encourage others to be leaders.

8

The Virtuous School

"The *virtuous* school? Don't you mean the *effective* school?" I imagine that many readers will react this way to the title of this chapter. In an age when technical rationality is prized and instrumental definitions of effectiveness are taken for granted as the goal for schooling, it seems odd to talk about the virtuous school. Happily, however, the two are connected. Although virtue is a justifiable end in its own right, the evidence from research on school effectiveness (Edmonds, 1979; Brookover and Lezotte, 1979) and school culture (Deal, 1987; Sergiovanni, 1984; Lipsitz, 1984) increasingly suggests that effective schools have virtuous qualities that account for a large measure of their success.

Focus Schools

The research on school effectiveness and school culture is buttressed by a recent RAND Corporation study, appropriately titled *High Schools with Character* (Hill, Foster, and Gendler, 1990). The researchers studied ten high schools in New York City and three in Washington, D.C. All were inner-city schools and served students drawn from a pool of severely disadvantaged young people. In every case, the focus schools were either Catholic or public magnet schools; zoned schools were regular public neighborhood schools. School effectiveness was determined in part from interviews of students, students' responses to a survey instrument assessing school climate and other factors, graduation rates, percentage of students taking the SAT, SAT scores, and the researchers' impressions of in-depth interviews.

"Focus" urban high schools were much more effective in serving disadvantaged students in New York City and Washington, D.C., than the "zoned" schools were in serving similar populations: "Focus schools resemble one another, and differ from zoned comprehensive public schools in two ways. First, focus schools have clear uncomplicated missions centered on the experiences [they intend] to provide [their] students and on the [way they intend] to influence [their] students' performance, attitudes and behavior. Second, focus schools are strong organizations with a capacity to initiate action in pursuit of their missions, to sustain themselves over time, to solve their own problems, and to manage their external relationships" (Hill, Foster, and Gendler, 1990, p. vii). Further, "their distinct characters set them apart, in the minds of their staff, students, and parents from other schools. . . each has a special identity that inspires a sense of loyalty and common commitment. They are committed to education in its broadest sense, the development of whole students. They induce values, influence attitudes and integrate diverse sources of knowledge. They also transmit facts and impart skills, but mainly they try to mold teenagers into responsible, productive adults" (pp. 55–56).

The focus schools concentrated all their efforts and energies on their conceptions of what students should be and know. They had strong social contracts that communicated the reciprocal responsibilities of administrators, teachers, and students. They made clear to everyone what the benefits would be of fulfilling this contract faithfully. They had a strong commitment to parenting and worked hard to mold students' attitudes and values. They had "centripetal curricula" that drew all students toward learning a common set of course skills and perspectives.

The zoned schools, by contrast, emphasized delivering instructional and other service programs to students and following procedures. Instead of relying on strong social contracts, they allowed staff and students to define their own roles. They saw themselves primarily as transmitters of information and imparters of skills. Finally, they emphasized the tracking of students and offered a potpourri of curricular options, in an effort to find something for everyone. The emphasis seemed to be more on processes and treatments than on the substance of purposes, people, and outcomes. These characteristics gave the schools a diffuse and ambiguous sense of identity as technical and instrumental organizations, rather than self-contained, freestanding entities.

From the organizational perspective, the focus schools operated as problem-solving organizations. They were free to take whatever initiatives were necessary to make things work. They worked hard to protect and sustain their distinctive character by attracting like-minded staff members and socializing new teachers and students to what the school was about. Finally, they considered themselves accountable to parents, students, and parish groups. Zoned schools, by contrast, operated in response to external mandates, had little freedom to select staff and scant inclination to influence the attitudes of new staff members, and answered primarily to bureaucratic superiors. Three factors seemed particularly important in accounting for the difference: a clear sense of purpose that comprised a common rallying point for what was done and why; a social contract that connected members to school purposes and shared values in a covenantal way; and site-based management, which the researchers found crucially important but not sufficient in itself to make the difference. Autonomy over budgets, schedules, educational programs, hiring, and other factors was effective only if it directly facilitated the establishment of purpose and social contract.

It is no secret that the norms of the student subculture can often force students to behave in ways that they might not choose otherwise. Black students who study are often punished by their peers for acting "white"; being cool means fast-lane engagement in sex, drinking, and so on; it's okay to make the grade by using charm, but if you use your brains, you are a nerd. Social contracts, linked to purposing, are powerful tools for establishing within the school a norm system that is more powerful than the one associated with the student subculture. Once in place, this norm system can be a safe haven that enables students to be themselves. It becomes okay to cooperate, to study, to be civil, and so on. According to Sister Justina Daley of Notre Dame Academy, Worcester, Massachusetts, "In some schools it isn't, as they say, 'cool' to study or want to learn or to be interested in advanced-level subjects. Here it is all right to be interested in courses like advanced-level modern language or French V, and I think the kids feel quite assured by it" (cited in the *Telegram and Gazette*, 1990, p. 6).

Building a Covenant

When purpose, social contract, and local school autonomy become the basis of schooling, two important things happen. The school is transformed from an organization to a covenantal community, and the basis of authority changes, from an emphasis on bureaucratic and psychological authority to moral authority. To put it another way, the school changes from a secular organization to a sacred organization, from a mere instrument designed to achieve certain ends to a virtuous enterprise.

In the discussion of purposing that appeared in Chapter Six, the concept of the covenant was introduced as being able to provide the kind of morally based contractual relationship that can bond people together. Bonding relationships respond to the reality that emotion, values, and membership connections are important human impulses. They also acknowledge the aspect of human nature that places other interests before self-interest. Finally, they give needed meaning and significance to our work lives. These inclinations join covenant and virtue. It is difficult to talk about school covenants without also concerning oneself with what comprises the virtuous school.

I recently participated in a Phi Delta Kappa seminar held at the Gene Autry Western Museum in Los Angeles. During a break in the meeting, I toured the museum and came across two displays that suggested metaphors for the virtuous school. One, depicting a Mormon group, was titled "A Covenantal Community." The placard describing it read as follows: "A covenantal community is a group of people who share religious or ethical beliefs, feel a strong sense of place, and think that the group is more important than the individual." The second, showing a pioneer family moving west, was titled simply "The Family." Families are covenantal communities of a special kind. The placard describing the display read this way: "The family has always been one of the most important kinds of communities. Families inspire deep loyalty. Family members work together and benefit one another, supplying economic and social needs. Tradition and social rules are passed along from parents to children." Covenants are solemn and binding agreements between two or more parties that provide reciprocal rights, duties, and obligations on the one hand, and guidelines for action, on the other. They define how one should live as an individual and one's collective life as a member of the community.

The covenantal relationships of the Mormons, the family, and other known communities are already established. But what should be the substance of the school's covenant, the school's center of purposes and shared values? Since Aristotle, philosophers have sought answers to the question of how we should live our lives as individuals and as members of collectivities. This issue will not be resolved in just a few paragraphs, or in a single chapter of a book. Our purpose here, then, is not to resolve the issue but to help school leaders begin a conversation that can help school communities grapple with the issue.

Some readers may find the following analysis too practical, but the intent is to provide some rules of thumb that teachers, parents, students, and administrators can use to help decide whether a certain norm, value, or belief should be part of the school's covenant. What follows, therefore, is not philosophical discourse, in the tradition of the discipline, but ordinary reasoning. Kant (1959), writing in 1785, observed that "the most remarkable thing about ordinary reason in its practical concern is that it may have as much hope as any philosopher of hitting the mark. In fact, it is almost more certain to do so than the philosopher, because he has no principle which the common understanding lacks, while his judgment is easily confused by a mass of irrelevant considerations, so that it easily turns aside from the correct way" (p. 21). Let us hope that Kant is correct in this case.

Figure 8.1. Moral and Managerial Imperatives.

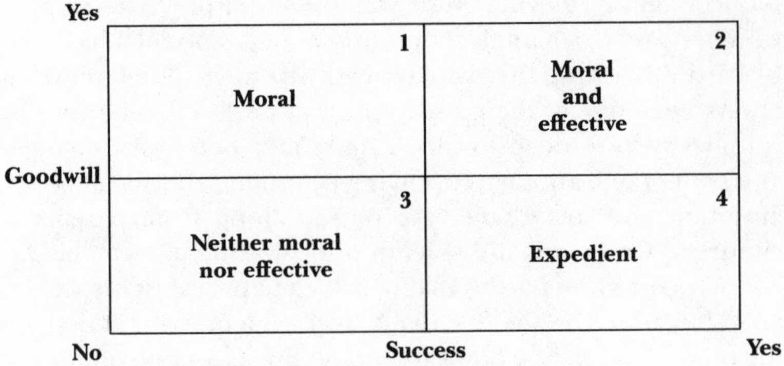

The Moral Imperative

Before we begin the search for some simple rules, we must discuss the concept of moral and managerial imperatives. The term *moral imperative* refers to what is good; the term *managerial imperative*, to what works. Kant pointed out that for any action or decision to have moral worth, it must be done from duty. Duty in turn is connected to some conception of what is good. Morally speaking, whether or not an action succeeds in accomplishing some instrumental end is irrelevant; what counts is whether one is motivated by goodwill. Practically speaking, the virtuous school seeks to operate on the basis of both what is good and what is effective. Nevertheless, there is a difference between actions that meet both these requirements and those that are merely expedient.

Figure 8.1 is composed of two dimensions, goodwill and success. Quadrant 1, where a person is motivated by goodwill but is not successful in achieving goals, is still considered moral. Quadrant 4, where one is not motivated by goodwill but is successful in achieving goals, is not considered moral but rather expedient. By one measure, it is successful; by another, it is not.

In quadrant 4, a principal may successfully use a style of leadership that makes teachers feel important and involved, not because they or their contributions are valued but because the principal believes that, as a result of their involvement, teachers will be easier to manipulate. In quadrant 1, by contrast, a principal who wants two new teachers to remain at the school gives the same support and help to the one who is leaving as to the one who is staying. Time spent in helping the first teacher could be viewed as time used ineffectively, for it represents time lost to the second teacher; but, morally speaking, intentions count for more than effectiveness does.

One could reason that, in the long run, quadrant 1 leads to quadrant 2. Like individuals, schools can be thought of as having character. Tending to the developmental needs of the departing teacher can help to strengthen this character. One result may be that the school's reputation for integrity and goodwill is enhanced. One could argue that this standing in the eyes of others puts the school in a better position to achieve its goals over time. The more that effectiveness is emphasized in the short run, the less likely it is that the school will actually be effective in the long run.

Ideally, the virtuous school strives to operate from within quadrant 2. This is the quadrant that seems best to embody schools with "character" (Hill, Foster, and Gendler, 1990). It also seems to fit the image of schools that emerges from the literature on effective schools and school culture.

Moral Principles

The distinctions between goodwill and success are important because even though schools have instrumental purposes, the fundamental basis of any covenantal relationship should be moral. With that in mind, we need now to decide on some moral principles that can be considered good in and of themselves — principles that can guide what we do, without regard to instrumental value. Two worth considering are proposed by the contemporary philosopher William K. Frankena (1973): the principle of justice and the principle of beneficence.

The principle of justice is expressed as equal treatment of and respect for the integrity of individuals. Accepting this principle means that every parent, teacher, student, administrator,

and other member of the school community must be treated
with the same equality, dignity, and fair play. The principle of
beneficence is expressed as concern for the welfare of the school
as a community. Accepting this principle means that every
parent, teacher, student, and administrator is viewed as an interdependent member of the school as covenantal community and
that every action taken in the school must seek to advance the
welfare of this community.

    If these two principles are accepted, what will be reason-
able tests of whether a norm, value, or purpose should be
included in the school's covenant? Three somewhat related tests
are worth considering: Kant's (1959) "second categorical imperative," John Rawls's (1971) "veil of ignorance," and the moment of
empathy derived from Jurgen Habermas's (1990) "discourse
ethics."

    Kant's second categorical imperative is simply stated: "Act
so that you treat humanity, whether in your own person or in
that of another, always as an end and never as a means only"
(p. 47). This rule should comprise the first test to be applied in
considering a course of action or adopting a set of values for the
school. No matter how tempting it may be to use other people
for one's own purposes, this rule requires that we act otherwise.
Were this rule to reign in the world of leadership, much of the
existing literature on the topic (based on the purpose of leadership as getting others to do what the leader wants and like it in
the bargain) would need to be scrapped. Leaders would still
exert influence and try to make things happen, but the authority
for what they do would not be the clever use of psychological
skills; it would be the substance of ideas, values, and commitments. Leaders would have to be more open in their intentions
and more forthright in their means. Kenneth Benne (1949)
suggests that the required openness and forthrightness can
come from basing one's attempts to influence others on four
basic principles: collaboration, educational benefits, experimentation, and task orientation. Collaboration implies that
leaders and the led form a change partnership, with each side
being aware of the intentions of the other. Leaders are honest
and straightforward with respect to what changes are sought

and the purpose of interactions with the led. (Teachers would not have to endure being "buttered up" so that they would be more likely to accept a change imposed on them.) The principle of educational benefits requires the process of change itself to help teachers become better problem solvers and better self-managers and therefore become less dependent on their leaders in the future. Over the long term, the leader's influence should not be directed at providing teachers with answers or solutions but rather with helping them invent their own answers and solutions. The principle of experimentation should make clear to teachers that attempts to influence are not intended to cause inflexible, permanent changes but rather resilient changes, which can be reshaped by new evidence and changed if necessary. The principle of task orientation involves the leader's motives for attempting to influence others. The leader has school purposes and job-related objectives in mind as primary reasons for seeking to change things, not her or his own self-interest.

Rawls (1971) believes that just principles are those that people choose in a hypothetical position of fairness while under a "veil of ignorance." When we are under the veil, it is assumed, we do not know anything about ourselves—that is, we do not know whether we are students, teachers, administrators, or parents. We do not know what our race or sex is, what our talents are, or what our position is in the hierarchical structure of the school. Rawls proposes that if we do not know who we will turn out to be until the "veil of ignorance" is lifted, we will fashion principles and make decisions regardless of our self-interest. With self-interest aside, principles would be fairer and more just. We would insist, Rawls reasons, that our own interests are best served by providing for a just distribution of rights, duties, and benefits.

The "moment of empathy" (Habermas, 1990) works this way. In conversation with others, each parent, principal, student, teacher, or other member of the community puts herself or himself in the place of everyone else in order to discuss whether a norm is fair enough for everyone to accept. Rawls assumes that we adopt a posture of not knowing our own role and then decide; Habermas proposes not only that we do know our role but also that we get into everyone else's.

Taken together, the tests of Kant, Rawls, and Habermas can help school community members come to grips with their purposes and shared values, on the one hand, and with designing the management systems, organizational arrangements, and other instrumental means needed to turn them into realities, on the other.

Frankena (1973), defining morality, says, "We are referring to a code or a set of moral beliefs rather than to a pattern or quality of conduct as character—to something a person or society *has* or subscribes to, rather than something he, she or it *is* or *does*" (p. 17). He continues, "A morality is a normative system in which evaluative judgments of some sort are made, more or less consciously, from a certain point of view, namely, from the point of view of a consideration of the effects of actions, motives, traits, etc., on the lives of persons or sentient beings as such, including the lives of others besides the person acting, being judged, or judging" (p. 26). Finally, as morality affects individuals, "to have a morality one must accept, believe in, or subscribe to, and judge by, some moral value system or other, though it need not actually be very systematic" (p. 28).

The heart of the school as moral community is its covenant of shared values. This covenant provides a basis for determining its morality. Up to this point, we have discussed two forms of this morality—one defined by what it means to be a professional, and the other defined by the norms that define the school as covenantal community. The virtuous school subscribes to and uses these moralities as a basis for deciding what its values are and how they will be pursued.

In many respects, school covenants are similar to mindscapes for individuals. They represent a collective world view that has both basic and temporal qualities. At the basic level, this world view, according to Benjamin (1990), is composed of a complex and interlocking set of deeply held and cherished beliefs about the nature and structure of the universe and one's place in it. Among its elements are deep convictions about the nature and purposes of human existence; conceptions of knowledge and our capacity to acquire it; the nature of human beings (our capacity, for example, to exercise free will, goodness, self-lessness, and compassion); best ways to structure human relationships; and definitions of morality. At the temporal level, this collective world view encompasses deeply held conceptions of how schools work; the nature of human motivation, power, and authority; how decisions are made; assumptions of how students learn, grow, and develop; and the nature of the process of schooling itself. These elements comprise the subject matter for covenant building.

Guidelines for Deciding

There is no easy answer to the difficult question of covenant building in large schools characterized by diverse points of view. Private schools can handle the problem by publicly declaring their purposes and values. They can then hire teachers who agree and recruit like-minded families by relying on the mechanism of choice. The relationship is not entirely one-sided, for parents and teacher have a say in shaping purposes and values. Public schools, by contrast, generally have little control over the teachers to be employed or the families to be served. One option is for them to build, within the larger school, smaller communities that function as semiautonomous schools. A high school of two thousand students, for example, could function as several smaller schools under the same roof.

It is important to point out that schools without covenants—schools that fit the image of organizations, rather than that of communities—still follow some moral code. Granted that the code may be implicit; nevertheless, "everyone who makes a decision relies on a moral code, shifting though it may be" (Guy, 1990, p. 6). For this reason, Guy believes, a publicly stated moral code that is conscientiously applied is the best way to ensure that decisions maximize important values.

In our democratic society, it is generally acknowledged that we all have rights that exist independently of our connections with government, school, the community, and other groups. Ruggiero (1988) points out that one fundamental right is to be treated with respect and be left alone, "as long as one does not infringe on others' rights" (p. 28). But life is complex, and rights are always mixed together with responsibilities; one compromises the other. To help resolve this tension, Ruggiero offers four additional working principles, to be considered along with the first:

1. Relationships with other people create *obligations* of various kinds, and these should be honored unless there is compelling reason not to do so. There are, for example, formal agreements or contracts, obligations of family membership (parent to child, child to parent, husband to wife, and vice versa), obligations of friendship, employer-employee obligations, and business and professional obligations.

2. Certain *ideals* enhance human life and assist people in fulfilling their obligations to one another. These should be served whenever possible. Among the most important ideals are . . . tolerance, compassion, loyalty, forgiveness, peace, brotherhood, justice (giving people their due), and fairness (being impartial, as opposed to favoring selected people).

3. The *consequences* of some actions benefit people, while those of other actions harm people. The former actions should be preferred over the latter. Consequences, of course, can be emotional as well as physical, momentary as well as lasting, and subtle as well as obvious.

4. *Circumstances* alter cases. Generalizations have their place, but too often they are used as a substitute for careful judgment. . . . Good thinking about issues means getting beyond generalizations and examining the particulars of the case [p. 28].

When obligations are in conflict, Ruggiero says, we should struggle to decide which is the most serious one. When ideals are in conflict, we should ask which is the highest or most important.

Examples

Beyond the absolutes already implied in the tests of Kant, Rawls, and Habermas, covenants must be built from the bottom up, as each school (or school within the school) strives to complete the transformation from organization to community.

The Appleton, Wisconsin, School District has chosen to begin the process of building a covenant by defining its core leadership values (see Appendix A). Statements of values are intended to provide direction and inform decisions, but this does not always happen easily. One solution to the problem of making value statements operational is to translate them into decision-making guidelines. This strategy, however, can sometimes result in guidelines that become scripts. As scripts, they contradict the very values they are supposed to embody. Appleton's statements suggest that the district is struggling with the problem of finding the right balance.

Two more examples are drawn from the Peel (Ontario) Board of Education, and the Center for Creative Leadership, Greensboro, North Carolina (see Appendix B, Appendix C). Peel began its process by developing a vision for the school system for the year 2000. This forecast provided a means of linking the district's core values with a delineation of issues to be addressed, the direction to be taken, and plans to get there. The Center for Creative Leadership's values constitute the defining core of the center's covenant. The center chose to vividly describe what it believes and why, leaving the decision guidelines to emerge in use.

Appendix D (Clark and Meloy, 1989) is based on a deep commitment to democratic values and represents a vision for constructing a new school that shares this commitment.

A Personal Perspective

The following are examples of characteristics that I believe should be included in the covenant of the virtuous school:

1.   The virtuous school believes that, to reach its full potential in helping students learn, it must become a learning community in and of itself. It is therefore committed to developing a spirit of curiosity, inquiry, and reflection that touches adults and students alike. The goal of the virtuous school is to create self-learners and self-managers. Each day, students depend a little less on their teachers and the school. Each day students rely a little more on their own convictions and resources. Each day, teachers rely a little less on their supervisors and administrators. Each day, teachers rely a little more on their own convictions and resources.

2.   The virtuous school believes that every student can learn, and it does everything in its power to see that every student does learn. Learning conditions that impede learning, no matter what their origins, are viewed as problems to be solved, rather than as conditions to be accepted.

3.   The virtuous school seeks to provide for the whole student. Although it is essentially academic, it recognizes that problems of learning are systemic. Therefore, the virtuous school does not shrink from its responsibility to do everything in its power to attend to the developmental, physical, and social needs of its students. Prime among its values is the ethic of caring, and caring is viewed as a key to academic success.

4.   The virtuous school honors respect. The virtuous school respects teachers by acknowledging both their professional commitment and their knowledge of craft. Teachers are free to decide for themselves what and how to teach and, in other ways, to express their own personal visions of teaching. Teachers respond to such acknowledgment by accepting responsibility for conducting themselves in accordance with the professional ideal. The virtuous school respects students by giving them the same consideration given to teachers, parents, and other adults. The result is a pattern of mutual respect, involving teachers with teachers and teachers with students, that increases the likelihood that teachers and students will respect themselves.

5.   In the virtuous school, parents, teachers, community, and school are partners, with reciprocal and interdependent rights to participate and benefit and with obligations to support and assist. It is recognized that the school needs the advice and support of parents if its work in teaching and learning is to be meaningful and effective. By the same token, parents need the advice and support of the school if their work in parenting is to be meaningful and effective. By involving parents constructively, the school can become more constructively involved with students. By involving the school constructively, parents can become more constructively involved with their own children. The word *parity* is a key here, for it communicates a relationship of mutual trust and goodwill, as well as mutual benefits.

The characteristics that I propose can serve as a rationale for developing a policy structure for the virtuous school. For example, schools are concerned, in one way or another, with discipline, and many find it helpful to develop policies that help clarify what should be done about it. What would a discipline policy look like in the virtuous school that I describe? To begin with, the school would be committed to a policy of nonaggression and nonviolence. Believing that violence begets violence, the school would take the stance that both initiated violence and routine retaliatory violence are unacceptable. New York City's Central Park East Secondary School provides a model for this value. Describing the school, its codirector, Paul Schwarz, comments, "People do not expect violence. Students feel safe. There are strict rules about violence and everyone seems to believe that they are going to be obeyed. . . [the school] is not a place where people are worried about physical or verbal violence" (cited in Hechinger, 1990, p. B14). At Central Park East, "The rules are clear. No fighting, not even 'play fighting.' No threats of fighting or fighting back on or off school grounds. The only exception allows a student to fight back if his or her life is threatened" (Hechinger, 1990, p. B14). It is more than rules that count; the rules have to be accepted and enforced by the entire school community. Further, they do not work unless they are accompanied by the right climate: "Our main decision was to create a coherent program focused on teaching kids to use their minds well. To do so, we decided we needed a staff who knew the kids well — that is, small classes and a low teacher-pupil ratio" (Central Park East director Deborah Meier, cited in Hechinger, 1990, p. B14). The net effect was to create a school climate characterized by a close, trusting relationship among students and between students and adults: "When young people are not anonymous, they shed antisocial behavior, including violence" (Hechinger, 1990, p. B14).

Key to Central Park East's success is its commitment to personalization and to engaging students and teachers in a familylike atmosphere. Teacher Herb Rosenfeld explains: "At my other school, I used to walk past two kids rolling around on the floor, having a fight. That wasn't my business. That was up to the security guards or whomever. That sort of situation doesn't happen at CPESS. First of all, we have maybe five fights a year, because we have a school focus on non-violence and conflict resolution. But, setting that aside, everything that happens is *everybody's* business. After all, in your house, if your kids are acting crazy, your husband doesn't wait until you get home. It makes sense to do certain things, and it's easy if your model is the elementary school classroom where what you're learning is the first issue" (cited in Lockwood, 1990, p. 9).

Even in the best of climates, simply laying down a set of rules will not do. Rules should be viewed and understood as a constitution, which comes complete with a rationale shared with students and other members of the school community. This constitution, as Seymour Sarason (1990) suggests, should answer the question "How should we live together as members of a community, and why?" Answering requires students to help construct the constitution in the first place and to have opportunities to voice their opinions about it, even offering amendments from time to time.

Beyond policies, the characteristics of virtue that I propose imply the kinds of attitudes that would govern day-to-day decision making. For example, the virtuous school would emphasize risk taking and would be accepting of reasonable failure. Further, it would encourage teachers and others to "reinvent the wheel." Conventional wisdom encourages a different attitude: Why should we struggle with developing our own system of teacher evaluation or our own curriculum guidelines, when they already exist or are commonly available in other school districts? Better to avoid risk and stick with what has been proved to work elsewhere.

Reinventing the wheel does not mean ignoring existing research or other pertinent evidence, but it does allow teachers to construct for themselves applications to practice. Superintendent Joanne Yatvin (1990) used to follow the risk-avoidance script; nowadays, however, she is "not so compliant. Maybe that's because I have become an old hand myself and an administrator to boot. But I prefer to think it is because I have learned something along the way: You have to reinvent the wheel whether you want to or not because nobody else's wheel will work on your wagon" (p. 25). The reasons Yatvin gives are the Hawthorne effect (when people believe their talents are valued and they are important, everything works; when they do not, nothing works) and the enhancement of craft knowledge. Through reinvention, teachers' development and in-depth understanding are enhanced; they are able to fine tune what they learn; they are able to adapt it to new situations, and their teaching practice improves because "a big part of teaching is inventing."

The characteristics that I propose also support a specific kind of attitude toward what leadership is and how it works. In the virtuous school, the leader would be seen as a servant. As Robert K. Greenleaf (1977) points out, people's caring for one another is the foundation on which a good society is built. One dimension of professional virtue is the caring ethic. Caring places teachers and administrators in service to others. Greenleaf believes that it is becoming increasingly difficult to support the imperative to care, person to person. For this reason, the caring ethic is mediated more and more by society's institutions: churches, schools, and business. As servant, the school fully accepts its responsibility to do everything it can to care for the full range of needs of its students, teachers, and parents. Further, it believes its academic responsibilities can be accomplished only through its stance of servant.

When respect for all is taken seriously, leadership is forced into the servant mode. One way to show respect is to serve another person. This idea seems less troublesome when it is applied to teachers, rather than to students, but its full embodiment is in serving students. Students are served in many ways. One way to respect and serve them is to share time with them. Since time is a scarce resource, how it is used communicates powerful messages.

Mary Helen Rodriguez, principal of De Zavala School, San Antonio, Texas, uses time to serve and respect (Albritton, 1991). She was interviewed recently by two third-grade students, who were researching the history of De Zavala School; her having taken time for this activity is worth noting. One of the students asked Rodriguez who the first Hispanic principal of De Zavala was. She did not know and could not find the answer in her files. With the students waiting, Rodriguez spent the next twenty minutes on the phone with various people at the central office, trying to get an answer. As Albritton explains, "One way to spell respect is TIME; that the principal would take time out of her busy day to track down the answer to a couple of students' questions sends a clear message that those students and their questions are important" (p. 3).

In many ways, respect is a form of empowerment. It invites people to accept higher levels of responsibility for their own behavior and for the school itself. When we feel that we count, we are more likely to take an interest in what is going on. This is what happened to students at De Zavala School when they noticed graffiti on the walls. Seventeen third-graders sent the following letter to Mrs. Rodriguez (Albritton, 1991, p. 4).

April 8, 1991

Dear Mrs. Rodriguez:
 We have a problem here at De Zavala. It's outside on our jungle gym. Our problem is that someone has written bad language on our jungle gym. We are afraid that little kids will catch on and learn from it. Also this doesn't represent our school well. It's ruining our reputation.
 We've thought about it a lot and we want to ask your permission to ask Mr. _____ to use his secret cleaner to clean it off and solve our problem. We'd

like to help or at least watch him do the job. We really want this taken care of, so we are all signing our names to this request. Thank you for your help.

Sincerely,

Servant leadership can be much more powerful than other forms. When we are served, our response is largely governed by our emotions and connections (themes to be elaborated on in Chapter Nine).

Many other qualities could be listed for the virtuous school. For example, the virtuous school respects diversity. In evaluating teachers, it stresses uniformity with respect to duties and obligations but honors differences in teaching style and personality preferences. The virtuous school applies the tests of Kant, Rawls, and Habermas. The virtuous school provides a clean and safe environment for its members. The virtuous school invites participation from all members of the school community. Superintendent Michael Massorotti of Adams County, Colorado, summarizes this characteristic as follows: "If you are going to be affected by any decision, you are invited to participate in shaping it" (personal communication, 1991). The virtuous school gives as much attention to enablement as it does to empowerment; it considers the two to be interdependent parts of the same whole: People should have both discretion and whatever assistance they need to use it wisely. This characteristic applies equally to teachers, students, parents, and other members of the school community.

Having reviewed this list of characteristics and qualities, you probably agree with some, would modify others, and find some unacceptable. This leads to the prime question: What is your vision for the virtuous school? Moreover, what is the collective vision of your school — the center that makes your school a covenantal community? Barth (1990, p. 148) suggests completing such sentences as "When I leave this school, I would like to be remembered for. . ." and "I want my school to become a place where. . ." and "The kind of school I would like my children to attend would. . ." and "The kind of school I would like to teach in. . ." Further, you could consider adopting, as a preamble to your vision for the virtuous school, the six principles that Ernest

Boyer (1990, p. 2) proposes for defining the kind of community that a university should strive to become: "An educationally purposeful community, an open community where freedom of expression... and civility are powerfully affirmed, a just community where the sacredness of the person is honored, a disciplined community where individuals accept their obligations to the group, a caring community, a celebrative community... where rituals affirming tradition and change are widely shared."

In describing the disconnectedness that seems to plague life in schools, Deal (1987) says, "Students find meaning in their subcultures. Teachers find meaning in unions and friends. Principals derive meaning from modern management ideologies and promotions. Superintendents dream of finding meaning in a larger district. Parents anchor their meaning in family and work, and on it goes across different groups—individual islands with no common glue to tie them together" (p. 11).

Expanding the bases of leadership practice to include moral bases, being concerned with the virtuous side of school life, and seeking to create covenantal communities in schools can help provide the measure of common meaning needed for schools to work and work well. As Superintendent Yatvin (1990, p. 25) puts it, "The only way to improve American education is to let schools be small, self-governing, self-renewing communities where everyone counts and everyone cares."

9

Leadership as Stewardship: "Who's Serving Who?"

Many school administrators are practicing a form of leadership that is based on moral authority, but often this practice is not acknowledged as leadership. The reason for this problem, as suggested in earlier chapters, is that moral authority is underplayed and that the management values undergirding this authority are largely unofficial. When I asked Larry Norwood, principal of Capital High School, Olympia, Washington, to participate in one of my studies on leadership, he responded, "I have wrestled with this—and finally decided to pass. First, because I am so late in responding and, second, I can think of nothing of literary significance that I have achieved (in the way of leadership) in the past twenty-two years. My style is to delegate and empower, and my successes have been through other people. If I have a strength it is as a facilitator—that doesn't make good copy. Sorry." Larry Norwood is a successful school administrator. Although he does not think of himself as a leader, he is one.

I suspect that one of the reasons for Norwood's success may be that he implicitly rejects leadership, as we now understand it. The official values of management lead us to believe that leaders are characters who singlehandedly pull and push organizational members forward by the force of personality, bureaucratic clout, and political know-how. Leaders must be decisive. Leaders must be forceful. Leaders must have vision. Leaders must successfully manipulate events and people, so that vision becomes reality. Leaders, in other words, must *lead*.

From time to time, there may be a place for this kind of direct leadership. But it is only part of the story. The leadership that counts, in the end, is the kind that touches people differently. It taps their emotions, appeals to their values, and responds to their connections with other people. It is a morally based leadership—a form of stewardship. Greenfield (1991) found this to be the case in his study of an urban elementary school. The moral orientation of its teachers was central in fixing their relationship with the principal and with each other. Greenfield comments, "Their persistence in searching out strategies to increase their colleagues' or their personal effectiveness in serving the needs of the school's children was motivated not by bureaucratic mandate or directives from superiors, but by moral commitment to children, rooted in their awareness of the needs of these children and their beliefs about the significance of their roles, as teachers, in these children's lives. Much of the principal's efforts to foster leadership among the teachers... was directed to further developing and sustaining this moral orientation among teachers" (p. 3). To those teachers, shared ideals and beliefs became duties to which they willingly responded. These findings parallel those of Johnson (1990). Morally based leadership is important in its own right, but it is also important because it taps what is important to people and what motivates them.

Stewardship in Practice

Implicit in traditional conceptions of leadership is the idea that schools cannot be improved from within: school communities have neither the wit nor the will to lead themselves; instead, principals and teachers are considered pawns, awaiting the play of a master or the game plan of an expert to provide solutions for school problems. In his chronicle of Madeline Cartwright, principal of Blaine School, Philadelphia, Richard Louv (1990) points out that too many teachers and administrators doubt the power of determination and the ability of schools themselves to make a difference. "It just won't work," they maintain, or "The central office won't let us," or "We can't do that because...."

Madeline Cartwright is one principal who thinks differently. For her, being a school administrator is a form of stewardship, and the responsibilities of stewardship simply require that obligations and commitments be met, regardless of obstacles. "I tell my staff don't tell me what I can and can't do. I can do something if I want to. It can happen. It's like people say to me, 'You cannot wash this child's clothes, put 'em in the washing machine and give him some clean clothes to put on.' I can do that" (p. 75). And that she does.

Shortly after becoming principal at Blaine, Cartwright organized a raffle to buy a washer and dryer for the school. They are used every morning, to launder the clothes of many of the children. Cartwright often does the washing personally, believing that this is the only way many of the children know what it is like to have clean clothes. In her words, "This is one of the things you can do to bring about a change. My kids look good" (p. 63). When Cartwright arrived at Blaine, she found a school that was "black as soot." She told the parents, "This place is dirty! How can your kids go to school in a place like this? We're going to clean this building this summer. Raise your hands if I can depend on you. Keep your hands up! Somebody get their names!" Eighteen parents showed up and began the work. "We cleaned it, and cleaned it good. I made these parents know that you don't accept anything less than that which is right because you live in North Philadelphia!" (p. 66).

Parental involvement at Blaine is high. Parents help supervise the yard in the morning and the hallway during the day. They work in classrooms, help prepare food, and decorate the school. "Everybody is involved in the washing" (p. 67).

What kind of leader is Madeline Cartwright? She is one who will do whatever it takes to make Blaine work and work well: "If a child isn't coming to school, I'll go into a home and bring kids out" (p. 74). On one such venture, Cartwright and a friend walked into an apartment she describes as follows: "This place was cruddy. I mean, beyond anything I could ever imagine for little children to live in. The kitchen was a hotplate sitting on a drainboard. I saw no refrigerator. There was no running water and no electricity. There were dirty dishes, food caked in piles.

The bathroom had a bedspread wrapped around the bottom of the toilet and the toilet was full to the brim with human waste. To the *brim*. And the little girl had one foot on one side of the toilet, and one foot on the other and she squatted over this toilet while she used it, and it was seeping over the sides." She sent one of the persons in the apartment off to get a snake. Then, using a plastic container and buckets from the school, "we dug this mess out. . . . While we were in the apartment, we scrubbed the floors, took all the dirty clothes out, all the sheets off the beds, brought them back to the school, washed them up. And we left food for dinner from our school lunch. The mother came home to a clean house and clean children. This lady had gotten so far behind the eight ball she didn't even know where to go to get out" (p. 74).

Some experts on the principalship might comment, "All well and good, but what about Cartwright's being an instructional leader? What about her paying attention to teaching and learning, to charting, facilitating, and monitoring the school's educational program?" Cartwright does that, all right, and with a flair. As Louv points out, Cartwright maintains that there are two types of principals, "office principals" and "classroom principals," and she is clearly the latter. She is in and out of classrooms regularly, often taking over the teaching of classes. She not only communicates high expectations but also demands performance from her staff. She is a no-nonsense disciplinarian, as well as a devoted and loving one. But all this "instructional leadership" just is not enough to make this school work. What makes Blaine work is that Cartwright practices leadership by washing clothes, scrubbing the building, and, yes, cleaning toilets (one of the chores that Mahatma Gandhi cheerfully claimed for himself as part of his leadership in the Indian independence movement). Both Cartwright and Gandhi were practicing something called *servant leadership*. In the end, it is servant leadership, based on a deep commitment to values and emerging from a groundswell of moral authority, that makes the critical difference in the lives of Blaine's students and their families. As Louv explains (p. 74), "Maybe Madeline Cartwright's dreams are naïve, maybe not. But they do make a kind of mathematical sense: one safe and clean school, one set of clean clothes, one clean toilet, one safe house — and then another safe school. . . and another. . . and another. 'I'm tellin' you, there's things you can do!'"

The Many Forms of Leadership

The practices of Madeline Cartwright and Larry Norwood demonstrate one of the themes of this book: leadership takes many forms. Further, as has been argued, today's crisis in leadership stems in part from the view that some of these forms are legitimate and others are not. For example, a vast literature expounds the importance of practicing command leadership and instructional leadership. Both kinds provide images of direct leadership, with the principal clearly in control — setting goals, organizing the work, outlining performance standards, assigning people to work, directing and monitoring the work, and evaluating. This kind of direct leadership is typically accompanied by a human relations style designed to motivate and keep morale up.

Command and instructional leadership have their place. Heavy doses of both may be necessary in schools where teachers are incompetent, indifferent, or just disabled by the circumstances they face. But if command and instructional leadership are practiced as dominant strategies, rather than supporting ones, they can breed dependency in teachers and cast them in roles as subordinates, with the consequences discussed in Chapter Six. Subordinates do what they are supposed to, but little else. They rely on others to manage them, rather than acting as self-managers. This is hardly a recipe for building good schools.

Command leaders and instructional leaders alike are being challenged by the view that school administrators should strive to become leaders of leaders. As leaders of leaders, they work hard to build up the capacities of teachers and others, so that direct leadership will no longer be needed. This is achieved through team building, leadership development, shared decision making, and striving to establish the value of collegiality. The leader of leaders represents a powerful conception of leadership, one that deserves more emphasis than it now receives in

the literature on school administration, and more attention
from policymakers who seek to reform schools. Successful leaders of leaders combine the most progressive elements of psychological authority with aspects of professional and moral
authority.

Servant Leadership

Virtually missing from the mainstream conversation on leadership is the concept of servant leadership—the leadership so
nobly practiced by Madeline Cartwright, Larry Norwood, and
many other principals. Greenleaf (1977) believes that "a new
moral principle is emerging which holds that the only authority
deserving one's allegiance is that which is freely and knowingly
granted by the led to the leader in response to, and in propor-
tion to, the clearly evident servant stature of the leader" (p. 10).
He developed the concept of servant leadership after reading
Herman Hesse's *Journey to the East*. As Greenleaf explains (p. 7),

> In this story we see a band of men on a mythical
> journey. . . . The central figure of the story is Leo,
> who accompanies the party as the servant who does
> their menial chores, but who also sustains them
> with his spirit and his song. He is a person of
> extraordinary presence. All goes well until Leo dis-
> appears. Then the group falls into disarray and the
> journey is abandoned. They cannot make it without
> the servant Leo. The narrator, one of the party,
> after some years of wandering, finds Leo and is
> taken into the Order that had sponsored the jour-
> ney. There he discovers that Leo, whom he had
> known first as servant, was in fact the titular head of
> the Order, its guiding spirit, a great and noble *leader*
> [p. 7].

For Greenleaf, the great leader is a servant first.
      Servant leadership is the means by which leaders can get
the necessary legitimacy to lead. Servant leadership provides

legitimacy partly because one of the responsibilities of leadership is to give a sense of direction, to establish an overarching
purpose. Doing so, Greenleaf explains, "gives certainty and
purpose to others who may have difficulty in achieving it for
themselves. But being successful in providing purpose requires
the trust of others" (p. 15). For trust to be forthcoming, the led
must have confidence in the leader's competence and values.
Further, people's confidence is strengthened by their belief that
the leader makes judgments on the basis of competence and
values, rather than self-interest.

When practicing servant leadership, the leader is often
tempted by personal enthusiasm and commitment to define the
needs of those to be served. There is, of course, a place for this
approach in schools; sometimes students, parents, and teachers
are not ready or able to define their own needs. But, over the
long haul, as Greenleaf maintains, it is best to let those who will
be served define their own needs in their own way. Servant
leadership is more easily provided if the leader understands
that serving others is important but that the most important
thing is to serve the values and ideas that help shape the school
as a covenantal community. In this sense, all the members of a
community share the burden of servant leadership.

In previous chapters, it was noted that schools should not
be viewed as ordinary communities but as communities of
learners. Barth (1990) points out that, within such communities,
it is assumed that schools have the capacity to improve themselves; that, under the right conditions, adults and students alike
learn, and learning by one contributes to the learning of others;
that a key leverage point in creating a learning community is
improving the school's culture; and that school-improvement
efforts that count, whether originating in the school or outside,
seek to determine and provide the conditions that enable students and adults to promote and sustain learning for themselves. "Taking these assumptions seriously," Barth argues
(pp. 45–46), "leads to fresh thinking about the culture of schools
and about what people do in them. For instance, the principal
need no longer be the 'headmaster' or 'instructional leader,'
pretending to know all, one who consumes lists from above and

transmits them to those below. The more crucial role of the principal is as head learner, engaging in the most important enterprise of the schoolhouse—experiencing, displaying, modeling, and celebrating what it is hoped and expected that teachers and pupils will do." The school as learning community provides an ideal setting for joining the practice of the "leader of leaders" to servant leadership.

Command and instructional leadership, "leader of leaders" leadership, and servant leadership can be viewed developmentally, as if each were built on the others. As the emphasis shifts from one level to the next, leadership increasingly becomes a form of virtue, and each of the preceding levels becomes less important to the operation of a successful school. For example, teachers become less dependent on administrators, are better able to manage themselves, and share the burdens of leadership more fully.

The developmental view is useful conceptually, but it may be too idealistic to account for what happens in practice. A more realistic perspective is to view the expressions of leadership as being practiced together. Initially (and because of the circumstances faced) the command and instructional features of the leadership pattern may be more prominent. In time, however (and with deliberate effort), they yield more and more to the "leader of leaders" style and to servant leadership, with the results just described.

The idea of servant leadership may seem weak. After all, since childhood, we have been conditioned to view leadership in a much tougher, more direct light. The media portray leaders as strong, mysterious, aloof, wise, and all-powerful. Lawrence Miller (1984) explains:

> Problems were always solved the same way. The Lone Ranger and his faithful Indian companion (read servant of a somewhat darker complexion and lesser intelligence) come riding into town. The Lone Ranger, with his mask and mysterious identity, background, and life-style, never becomes intimate with those whom he will help. His power is

partly in his mystique. Within ten minutes the Lone Ranger has understood the problem, identified who the bad guys are, and has set out to catch them. He quickly outwits the bad guys, draws his gun, and has them behind bars. And then there was always that wonderful scene at the end. The helpless victims are standing in front of their ranch or in the town square marveling at how wonderful it is now that they have been saved, you hear hoofbeats, then the *William Tell Overture*, and one person turns to another and asks, "But who was that masked man?" And the other replies, "Why, that was the Lone Ranger!" We see Silver rear up and with a hearty "Hi-yo Silver," the Lone Ranger and his companion ride away.

It was wonderful. Truth, justice, and the American Way protected once again.

What did we learn from this cultural hero? Among the lessons that are now acted out daily by managers are the following:

- There is always a problem down on the ranch [the school] and someone is responsible.
- Those who got themselves into the difficulty are incapable of getting themselves out of it. "I'll have to go down or send someone down to fix it."
- In order to have the mystical powers needed to solve problems, you must stay behind the mask. Don't let the ordinary folks get too close to you or your powers may be lost.
- Problems get solved within discrete periodic time units and we have every right to expect them to be solved decisively.

These myths are no laughing matter. Anyone who has lived within or close to our corporations [or schools] knows that these myths are powerful

forces in daily life. Unfortunately, none of them
bears much resemblance to the real world [pp.
54–55].

One way in which the servant leader serves others is by
becoming an advocate on their behalf. Mary Helen Rodriguez,
principal of San Antonio's De Zavala School, provides an
example:

A teacher came to Mrs. Rodriguez to discuss problems she had been having in arranging a field trip
for her grade level. The teacher, in reality, had
begun planning too late to get the bus and sack
lunch requests conveniently through the district
bureaucracy for the planned day of the trip. Mrs.
Rodriguez first asked the teacher how important
the field trip was for the students. After a bit of
discussion, Mrs. Rodriguez and the teacher decided that a trip to the zoo was indeed important,
given what students were studying in class at the
time. Mrs. Rodriguez then immediately set about
making the necessary preparations. Although it
took a bit of cajoling over the telephone, sack
lunches and busses were secured, and the teacher
was most appreciative.

The remarkable thing about this episode is
the extra effort Mrs. Rodriguez put in, even though
it would have been perfectly reasonable to say, "No,
I'm sorry. It's just too late." In a situation where
another principal might have saved her powder
and not fought the system, Mrs. Rodriguez proved
to be a successful advocate for the teacher and her
students [Albritton, 1991, p. 8].

Such ideas as servant leadership bring with them a different kind of strength—one based on moral authority. When one
places one's leadership practice in service to ideas, and to others
who also seek to serve these ideas, issues of leadership role and

of leadership style become far less important. It matters less who is providing the leadership, and it matters even less whether the style of leadership is directive or not, involves others or not, and so on. These are issues of process; what matter are issues of substance. What are we about? Why? Are students being served? Is the school as learning community being served? What are our obligations to this community? With these questions in mind, how can we best get the job done?

Practicing Servant Leadership

Embedded in the pages of this book are practices that, taken together, show how servant leadership works and how the burden of leadership can be shared with other members of the school community. They are summarized in the following sections.

Purposing

Vaill (1984) defines *purposing* as "that continuous stream of actions by an organization's formal leadership which has the effect of inducing clarity, consensus and commitment regarding the organization's basic purposes" (p. 91). The purpose of purposing is to build within the school a center of shared values that transforms it from a mere organization into a covenantal community. (See Chapter Six.)

Empowerment

Empowerment derives its full strength from being linked to purposing: everyone is free to do what makes sense, as long as people's decisions embody the values shared by the school community. When empowerment is understood in this light, the emphasis shifts away from discretion needed to function and toward one's responsibility to the community. Empowerment cannot be practiced successfully apart from enablement (efforts by the school to provide support and remove obstacles; see Chapter Eight).

Leadership by Outrage

It is the leader's responsibility to be outraged when empowerment is abused and when purposes are ignored. Moreover, all
members of the school community are obliged to show outrage
when the standard falls.

Leadership by outrage, and the practice of kindling outrage in others, challenge the conventional wisdom that leaders
should be poker-faced, play their cards close to the chest, avoid
emotion, and otherwise hide what they believe and feel. When
the source of leadership authority is moral, and when covenants
of shared values become the driving force for the school's norm
system, it seems natural to react with outrage to shortcomings in
what we do and impediments to what we want to do.

Madeline Cartwright regularly practiced leadership by
outrage. In one instance, she was having trouble with teachers'
attendance. She learned of another principal who solved this
problem by answering the phone personally, and she decided to
follow suit: "I started answering the phone. I say, 'Good morning,
this is the Blaine School, this is Madeline Cartwright.' They hang
right up. Two, three minutes later, phone rings again. 'Good
morning, this is Blaine School and still Madeline Cartwright.'
Hang right up. Next time the phone rang I said: 'Good morning,
this is Mrs. Cartwright. If you're going to take off today, you have
to talk to me. You either talk to me or you come to school, simple
as that'" (Louv, 1990, p. 64). The school is the only thing that the
kids can depend on, Cartwright maintains, and for this reason it
is important to make sure that the teachers will show up. She
tells the teachers, "As old as I am, you haven't had any disease I
haven't had, so you come to school, no matter what."

Some administrators who practice the art of leadership
by outrage do it by fighting off bureaucratic interference. Paperwork is often the villain. Other administrators capitulate and
spend much of their time and effort handling this paperwork.
As a result, little is left for dealing with other, more important
matters. Jules Linden, a junior high school principal in New
York City, and Linda Martinez, principal of San Juan Day
School, San Juan Pueblo, New Mexico, belong in the first group.

In Linden's words, "The only thing the bureaucracy hasn't tried to solve by memo is cancer. . . . My rule of thumb is, when people can't see me because of the paperwork demands, I dump [the paperwork]—and most of it is not missed" (Mustain, 1990, p. 14). Martinez has devised a unique filing system to handle the onslaught of memos, rules, directives, and the like, which she receives from above: "I decided to 'bag it.' Every Friday I would clear my desk. Everything would be tossed in a garbage bag, dated and labeled weekly." Should Martinez be contacted about something filed (and that is not often the case), the proper bag is opened and dumped on the floor, and the item is retrieved for further consideration. Linda Martinez remarks, "I had never really considered my 'filing system' of garbage bags to be associated with leadership. I've been told it borders on lunacy." In a redefined leadership, what first appears to be lunacy may not be, and vice versa.

Not all schools share the dire conditions of Blaine School, and not all are deluged with a mountain of paperwork. But every school stands for something, and this something can be the basis of practicing leadership by outrage. Many administrators and teachers believe that students do not have the right to fail— that, for example, it should not be up to students to decide whether to do assigned work. Unless this belief rests on the practice of leadership by outrage, however, it is likely to be an academic abstraction rather than a heartfelt value, a slogan rather than a solution.

How is failure to complete assigned work handled in most schools? Typically, by giving zeros—often cheerfully, and without emotion. It is almost as if we are saying to students, "Look, here is the deadline. This is what you have to do. If you don't meet the deadline, these are the consequences. It's up to you. You decide whether you want to do the assignments and pass, or not do the assignments and fail." Adopting a "no zero" policy and enforcing it to the limit is one expression of leadership by outrage. It can transform the belief that children have no right to fail from an abstraction to an operational value. When work is not done by Friday, for example, no zeros are recorded. Instead, the student is phoned Friday night, and perhaps the principal or the teacher visits the student at home after brunch on Sunday to collect the work or press the new Monday deadline. If the student complains that she or he does not have a place to do homework, homework centers are established in the school, in the neighborhood, and so on.

Just remember Madeline Cartwright, and follow her lead. Granted, not all students will respond, but I believe that most will, and those who finally do wind up with zeros will get them with teachers' reluctance. Even if the school does not "win them all," it demonstrates that it stands for something. The stakes are elevated when the problem is transformed from something technical to something moral.

As important as leadership by outrage is, its intent is to kindle outrage in others. When it is successful, every member of the school community is encouraged to display outrage whenever the standard falls. An empowered school community, bonded together by shared commitments and values, is a prerequisite for kindling outrage in others.

Power *Over* and Power *To*

It is true that many teachers and parents do not always respond to opportunities to be involved, to be self-managed, to accept responsibility, and to practice leadership by outrage. In most cases, however, this lack of interest is not inherent but learned. Many teachers, for example, have become jaded as a result of bad experiences with involvement. Louise E. Coleman, principal of Taft Elementary School, Joliet, Illinois, believes that trust and integrity have to be reestablished after such bad experiences. When she arrived at Taft as a new principal, the school was required to submit to the central office a three-year school-improvement plan, designed to increase student achievement:

> Teachers were disgruntled at first. They were not really interested in developing a school-improvement plan. They had been through similar exercises in shared decision making before, and that's exactly what they were — *exercises*. Taft had had three

principals in three years. The staff assumed that I would go as others had in the past. After writing a three-year plan based on the staff's perceptions, influencing teachers by involving them in decision making, helping them to take ownership in school improvement, [we have] made some progress. Trust and integrity have been established. Most of the staff now has confidence in me. We have implemented new programs based on students' needs. The staff now volunteers to meet, to share ideas. Minority students are now considered students. Communication is ongoing. Minority parents are more involved. Positive rewards are given for student recognition. The overall school climate has changed to reflect a positive impact on learning.

Coleman was able to build trust and integrity by gently but firmly allowing others to assume leadership roles. She did not feel too threatened to relinquish some of her power and authority. Power can be understood in two ways—as power *over*, and as power *to*. Coleman knows the difference. Power *over* emphasizes controlling what people do, when they do it, and how they do it. Power *to* views power as a source of energy for achieving shared goals and purposes. Indeed, when empowerment is successfully practiced, administrators exchange power *over* for power *to*. Power *over* is rule-bound, but power *to* is goal-bound. Only those with hierarchically authorized authority can practice power *over*; anyone who is committed to shared goals and purposes can practice power *to*.

The empowerment rule (that everyone is free to do whatever makes sense, as long as decisions embody shared values), and an understanding of power as the power *to*, are liberating to administrators as well as teachers. Principals, too, are free to lead, without worrying about being viewed as autocratic. Further, principals can worry less about whether they are using the right style and less about other process-based concerns; their leadership rests on the substance of their ideas and values. Contrary to the laws of human relations, which remind us always

to involve people and say that it is autocratic for designated
leaders to propose ideas for implementation, we have here a
game that resembles football: everyone gets a chance to be
quarterback and is free to call the play; if it is a good call, then
the team runs with it.

Wayne K. Myers, a principal in Madison, Georgia, wel-
comes teachers to the role of quarterback, but he is not afraid to
call some plays himself. In the spring of 1989, he declared one
week in August as International Week, having organized the
major activities on his own. He contacted parents for volunteers,
asked foreign students from the University of Georgia to come
to the campus and make presentations, arranged an exhibit
from UNICEF, and even asked the lunchroom to serve meals
from the cuisines of different countries:

> In describing this week, I keep [saying] "I" because
> the major activities were completed by me, but the
> real success of the week came from the teachers. It
> was based on a general understanding I had gained
> from working with these teachers: that they felt the
> true spirit of schooling had been lost, and that we
> were committed to recovering it. I shared my idea
> with them only one month before the start-up date.
> But, within that month, each grade organized a
> fantastic array of activities for students. The media
> specialist located all the materials she had on for-
> eign countries. The hallways were full of displays of
> items, made by the students, that represented other
> countries. Since each homeroom would have a vis-
> itor with information about another country, each
> teacher centered activities on that country. The real
> significance was that the general theme of the week
> may not have been [the teachers'] idea, but the
> response was unbelievable. They were, of course,
> free to take the idea and run with it. It became a
> learning experience for everyone—administrators,
> teachers, students, and the community. All were
> involved, and all enjoyed themselves. . . . I am not

> sure what type of leadership this is. All I know is
> that the results have been very positive. I do not
> believe in telling people what to do or how to do it,
> but I do believe that sometimes we all have ideas
> that need to be proposed, sometimes unilaterally.

Myers does not have to worry about leadership—that is, about who does what, or whether he is being too pushy or if he is passing the ball off to teachers. But he would have to worry if trust, integrity, and shared values were not already established in the school. Moreover, Myers understands the difference between charting a direction and giving people maps, between providing a theme and giving teachers a script. Finally, although human relations remain important, Myers is confident that if he acts from the standpoint of what is right and good for the school, human relationships will have a way of taking care of themselves.

The Female Style

It is difficult to talk about power *to* and servant leadership without also addressing the issue of gender. Power *to*, for example, is an idea close to the feminist tradition, as are such ideas as servant leadership and community. By contrast, the more traditional conceptions of leadership seem decidedly more male-oriented. Modern management, for example, is a male creation that replaced emphasis on family and community with emphasis on individual ambition and other personal considerations. As Debra R. Kaufman and Barbara L. Richardson (1982) explain, "Most contemporary social science models [of which modern school management is one]—the set of concepts that help social scientists select problems, organize information, and pursue inquiries—are based on the lives men lead." They go on to say, "In general, social science models of human behavior have focused on rather narrow and male-specific criteria regarding the relationships of ability, ambition, personality, achievement, and worldly success" (p. xiii).

Joyce Hampel (1988) argues that the concept of servant

leadership is not likely to be valued in male-dominated institutions or professions. Relying on the research of Carol Gilligan
(1982), Joyce Miller (1986), and Charol Shakeshaft (1987), as well
as on her own experiences in schools, Hampel points out that
men and women generally have different goals when it comes to
psychological fulfillment. Men tend to emphasize individual
relationships, individual achievement, power as a source for
controlling events and people, independence, authority, and set
procedures. Women, by contrast, tend to emphasize successful
relationships, affiliation, power as the means to achieve shared
goals, connectedness, authenticity, and personal creativity. For
most men, achievement has to do with the accomplishment of
goals; for most women, achievement has to do with the building
of connections between and among people. Hampel quotes
Miller as follows: "In our culture 'serving others' is for losers, it is
low-level stuff. Yet serving others is a basic principle around
which women's lives are organized; it is far from such for men"
(p. 18).

Shakeshaft (1987), in her groundbreaking research on the
topic, characterizes the female world of schooling as follows:

(1) *Relationships with Others Are Central to All
Actions of Women Administrators.* Women spend more
time with people, communicate more, care more
about individual differences, are concerned more
with teachers and marginal students, and motivate
more. Not surprisingly, staffs of women administrators rate women higher, are more productive,
and have higher morale. Students in schools with
women principals also have higher morale and are
more involved with student affairs. Further, parents
are more favorable toward schools and districts run
by women and thus are more involved in school
life. This focus on relationships and connections
echoes Gilligan's (1982) ethic of care.

(2) *Teaching and Learning Are the Major Foci of
Women Administrators.* Women administrators are
more instrumental in instructional learning than

men and they exhibit greater knowledge of teaching methods and techniques. Women administrators not only emphasize achievement, they co-
ordinate instructional programs and evaluate
student progress. In these schools and districts,
women administrators know their teachers and
they know the academic progress of their students.
Women are more likely to help new teachers and to
supervise all teachers directly. Women also create a
school climate more conducive to learning, one
that is more orderly, safer, and quieter. Not surprisingly, academic achievement is higher in schools
and districts in which women are administrators.

(3) *Building Community Is an Essential Part of a
Woman Administrator's Style.* From speech patterns to
decision-making styles, women exhibit a more democratic, participatory style that encourages in-
clusiveness rather than exclusiveness in schools.
Women involve themselves more with staff and students, ask for and get higher participation, and
maintain more closely knit organizations. Staffs of
women principals have higher job satisfaction and
are more engaged in their work than those of male
administrators. These staffs are also more aware of
and committed to the goals of learning, and the
members of the staffs have more shared professional goals. These are schools and districts in
which teachers receive a great deal of support from
their female administrators. They are are also districts and schools where achievement is emphasized. Selma Greenberg (1985, p. 4) describes this
female school world: "Whatever its failures, it is
more cooperative than competitive, it is more expe-
riential than abstract, it takes a broad view of the
curriculum and has always addressed 'the whole
child.'"

The female perspective on school leadership is important, for a number of reasons. The teaching force is predomi-

nantly female, and this raises moral questions about giving full
legitimacy to management conceptions and leadership practice
that take women's lived experience into account. Female principals need to feel free to be themselves, rather than have to
follow the principles and practices of traditional management
theory. The record of success for female principals is impressive.
Women are underrepresented in the principalship but over-
represented among principals of successful schools. Giving legitimacy to the female perspective would also give license to
men who are inclined toward similar practice. The good news is
that such ideas as value-based leadership, building covenantal
communities, practicing empowerment and collegiality, adopting the stance of servant leaders, and practicing leadership by
outrage are gaining in acceptance among male and female
administrators alike.

Servant Leadership and Moral Authority

The link between servant leadership and moral authority is a
tight one. Moral authority relies heavily on persuasion. At the
root of persuasion are ideas, values, substance, and content,
which together define group purposes and core values. Servant
leadership is practiced by serving others, but its ultimate purpose is to place oneself, and others for whom one has responsibility, in the service of ideals.

Serving others and serving ideals is not an either-or proposition. Chula Boyle, assistant principal of Lee High School, San
Antonio, Texas, for example, can often be seen walking the halls
of the school with a young child in arm or tow. Student mothers
at Lee depend on extended family to care for their children
while they are in school. When care arrangements run into
problems that might otherwise bar student mothers from at-
tending class, Boyle urges them to bring the children to school.
By babysitting, Boyle is serving students but, more important,
she reflects an emerging set of ideals at Lee. Lee wants to be a
community, and this transformation requires that a new ethic of
caring take hold. Lee High School Principal Bill Fish believes
that this type of caring is reciprocal. The more the school cares

about students, the more students care about matters of schooling. When asked about the practice of babysitting at Lee, he modestly responds, "From time to time kids get in a bind. We are not officially doing it [babysitting] but unofficially we do what we can." His vision is to establish a day-care center in the school for children of students and teachers.

One theme of this book is that administrators ought not to choose among psychological, bureaucratic, and moral authority; instead, the approach should be additive. To be additive, however, moral authority must be viewed as legitimate. Further, with servant leadership as the model, moral authority should become the cornerstone of one's overall leadership practice.

Stewardship

The "leader of leaders" and servant leadership styles bring stewardship responsibilities to the heart of the administrator's role. When this happens, the rights and prerogatives inherent in the administrator's position move to the periphery, and attention is focused on duties and responsibilities—to others as persons and, more important, to the school itself.

Stewardship represents primarily an act of trust, whereby people and institutions entrust a leader with certain obligations and duties to fulfill and perform on their behalf. For example, the public entrusts the schools to the school board. The school board entrusts each school to its principal. Parents entrust their children to teachers. Stewardship also involves the leader's personal responsibility to manage her or his life and affairs with proper regard for the rights of other people and for the common welfare. Finally, stewardship involves placing oneself in service to ideas and ideals and to others who are committed to their fulfillment.

The concept of stewardship furnishes an attractive image of leadership, for it embraces all the members of the school as community and all those who are served by the community. Parents, teachers, and administrators share stewardship responsibility for students. Students join the others in stewardship responsibility for the school as learning community. Mary

Giella, assistant superintendent for instruction in the Pasco County (Florida) Schools, captures the spirit of stewardship as follows: "My role is one of facilitator. I listened to those who taught the children and those who were school leaders. I helped plan what they saw was a need. I coordinated the plan until those participating could independently conduct their own plans."

The organizational theorist Louis Pondy (1978, p. 94) has noted that leadership is invariably defined as behavioral: "The 'good' leader is one who can get his subordinates to *do* something. What happens if we force ourselves away from this marriage to behavioral concepts? What kind of insights can we get if we say that the effectiveness of a leader lies in his ability to make activity meaningful for those in his role set — not to change behavior but to give others a sense of understanding what they are doing, and especially to articulate it so that they can communicate about the meaning of their behavior?"

This book has attempted to answer Pondy's questions. Shifting emphasis from behavior to meaning can help us recapture leadership as a powerful force for school improvement. Giving legitimacy to the moral dimension of leadership, and understanding leadership as the acceptance and embodiment of one's stewardship responsibilities, are important steps in this direction.

EPILOGUE

The Antidote
Can Become the Poison

Moral authority, emotion, social bonds, covenantal communities, duties and obligations, leadership by outrage — these represent dangerous ideas. On the one hand, they are strong medicine that, if used properly, can help us get to the heart of school improvement. On the other hand, the same strong medicine can encourage a leadership practice that is irrational, reactionary, and oppressive. The antidote can become the poison.

Social bonds, for example, can create norms within a school that become coercive, squashing individual thought and initiative and narrowing behavior by force of intimidation. Tapping emotion in seeking to motivate individuals and rally groups can give leaders an unfair advantage, if objective reasoning is sacrificed in the bargain. Covenants — initially struck by common agreement as means of serving students, and thought to be resilient — can become inflexible ideological statements that comprise ends in themselves; autocratic and even despotic leaders may emerge, who use covenants as bully pulpits. Worse yet, messianic leaders may emerge, who through deft charismatic manipulation of emotion are able to cultivate blind followership on the basis of poorly conceived ideas or a personal aura.

In all these cases, leader and led may become so committed to a set of ideas and a course of action that, like compulsive gamblers, they create an artificial reality that compels them to stay the course, when more detached evidence would indicate

141

that things are not working well or even that disaster is immi-
nent. Although moral leadership is designed to bring people
together in a common cause, for altruistic purposes, the dimensions of moral leadership may comprise the same ingredients
that create "systems of blood" that divide people.

Modern Beirut provides an apt metaphor. Marionite fac-
tions, Druse, numerous subgroups of Shiites, and Sunnis are all
primordially bonded into mutually antagonistic covenantal
communities. The leaders of these "tribes" rely heavily on creating and using particularistic moral authority in building followership. Such followership is constructed around a subjective
rationality within groups that is often considered irrational
(some would even say crazy) by more detached observers. The
result is that neither the various covenantal communities nor the
nation as a whole are served well.

Strong medicine is good medicine only when used properly. The ailment to be treated, it has been argued here, is
management theory and management practice that consider
logic, reason, scientific evidence, and bureaucratic authority to
be the only legitimate values of management and leadership.
The results have been the serious neglect of emotion and morality; the tendency to view individuals as rational, independent
actors, separated from group membership; a practice that considers self-interest to be the prime human motivator and that
neglects the importance and power of altruism and self-
sacrifice; and the viewing of leadership as a process involving
management and interpersonal skills, with scant regard for
substance and purpose.

The cure proposed here does not seek to replace the
values of traditional management theory and leadership practice but rather to expand them in a fashion that includes the
moral dimension. The moral dimension is far from all that
matters, but it does matter. Expanded theory and practice will
imply the acknowledgment of how messy administrative work is.

A good place to begin is to see administrative work as
characterized by pattern rationality. Jean Hills (1982) points out
that administrators rarely pursue goals one at a time, as if they
were discrete; they pursue several connected and often contra-

dictory goals at once. In an expanded theory of leadership, all the values that undergird administrative work must be viewed together, as a pattern. This pattern needs to be attended to as a whole, even though it changes from moment to moment. Like skillful surfers, administrators must figure out how to "ride the wave" of this pattern as it unfolds.

How can we be sure that the pattern of values not only includes the moral dimension but also avoids the negative consequences of unbalanced attention to this dimension? One idea worth considering is to legitimate the cultivation of a loyal opposition in matters of educational governance and administration, at all levels, from the individual school to the state capital. In a democracy, the loyal opposition is committed to the same overarching values as the majority, but differs in its views of how the values should be put into action and what the means of obtaining them should be. The relationship between majority and loyal opposition is characterized by mutual respect. In schools, the loyal opposition would furnish the necessary tension that stretches imagination, goodwill, and effectiveness on "both sides of the aisle" and would provide the checks and balances necessary to the protection of the overarching values.

Peter Block (1987) has given some thought to how a loyal opposition can make an enterprise better. He believes that, in working with a loyal opposition, it is important for majority leaders to communicate the extent to which the opposition is valued. This can be done by reaffirming the quality of the relationship and the fact that it is based on trust. Majority leaders must state their positions clearly, as well as the reasons why they hold them. Leaders should also state, in a neutral way, what they think the positions of the loyal opposition are. Leaders reason as follows: "We disagree with respect to purposes, goals, and perhaps even visions. Our task is to understand the opposition's position. Our way of fulfilling that task is to be able to state the opposition's arguments in a positive way. The opposition should feel understood and acknowledged by our statements of its disagreement with us." Perhaps with this kind of relationship, majority leaders and the loyal opposition can negotiate differences in good faith.

A final caveat has to do with the concept of leadership itself. Although it is common to do so, to elevate "leadership" and denigrate "management" is a mistake. One benefit of giving attention to ministering, servant leadership, and leadership as stewardship is that these conceptions redefine the routine, mundane, inspirational, and sense-making work of administration, so that all these aspects become interdependent and indistinguishable. When administrators "minister" to the needs of the school, what appears superficially to be managerial and routine communicates meaning in context. Schedules that work and overhead projectors with functioning bulbs are acknowledgments and celebrations of teaching's importance. Orderly, clean buildings become statements of pride and reflect regard for students. A common adage among administrators is that good management is a necessary but insufficient condition for successful leadership. Perhaps the point is better made in this way: "Good leadership is a necessary but insufficient condition for successful schooling."

APPENDIX A

Core Leadership Values: Appleton, Wisconsin, School District

Community

Belief Statement

The district should develop and nurture a sense of community among all members. *Community* means that all individuals working together share a commitment to understand and honor differing perceptions and concerns in an environment of trust.

Guidelines for Decision Making

1. The district will provide an atmosphere in which nonjudgmental listening and the opportunity to express opinions freely are encouraged.
2. The district will encourage shared problem solving at all levels.
3. The district will remove barriers to communication among all employee groups.
4. The district will invite frequent and active parental, business, community, student, and employee involvement in district issues.
5. The district will provide an environment that enables the individual to work in a professionally effective and personally healthy manner.

145

6. The district will acknowledge the existence of conflict and recognize that such conflict can be healthy if resolution is actively sought.
7. The district will continue to keep visible the feeling "we're all in this business together."

Quality

Belief Statement

Quality instruction and other related services to the students, employees, parents, and other publics should be the primary mission of our district.

Guidelines for Decision Making

1. The district will provide the necessary training to support quality instruction and other related services.
2. The district will eliminate barriers that prevent the delivery of quality instruction and other related services.
3. The district will provide incentives and opportunities for the continued professional growth and development of all employees.
4. The district will provide necessary instructional materials, equipment, and personnel to support all board-approved programs.
5. The district will follow recruitment, selection, and evaluation practices to employ and retain the highest-quality staff.
6. The district will support and enhance the quality of the work life of all employees by providing clean, safe, and inviting facilities.
7. The district will provide all students with equitable programs, facilities, and educational opportunities.
8. The district will expect ongoing quality improvement in service within our district and to our other publics.

Empowerment and Decision Making

Belief Statement

The power to make decisions and affect change should be distributed throughout the organizational structure of the district by providing the necessary support, information, and resources. Participatory decision making should be integral to the effective functioning of our school district.

Guidelines for Decision Making

1. The district will involve employees who have expertise and/or interest in decisions that are relevant to them (e.g., staffing, budgeting, curriculum, materials selection, and staff development).
2. The district will involve students, parents, and community representatives in the decision-making process, as appropriate.
3. The district will design organizational structures that encourage interaction beyond the typical departmental or school boundaries.
4. The district will seek, identify, and apply pertinent research regarding district decisions.
5. The district will train employees for leadership roles in the decision-making process.
6. The district will keep [its] publics informed on an ongoing basis during the decision-making process.
7. The district will encourage decisions to be made as close to the point of implementation as possible, with consideration being given to those accountable for that decision.
8. The district will recognize that individual employees must determine how they will prioritize commitments to best achieve both individual and organizational goals.

Risk Taking

Belief Statement

Risk taking and innovation should be supported as a way of achieving organizational improvement.

Guidelines for Decision Making

1. The district will encourage individuals and groups throughout the organization to initiate risk taking, innovation, and experimentation.
2. The district will create an atmosphere where people can make and acknowledge mistakes without fear of "failure."
3. The district will recognize individuals or groups for taking risks to further the mission of the district.
4. The district will recognize that short-term setbacks may in turn result in long-term personal and/or organizational growth.
5. The district will expect and support evaluation of experimental and innovative practices and encourage wider implementation of successful programs.
6. The district will encourage the sharing of results from experimental or innovative practices and programs, whether they are successful or not.
7. Conflict will be considered a sign of a healthy organization and will be resolved in a spirit of fairness, respect, and trust.
8. The district will encourage individuals with appropriate expertise to consider new assignments, even though these assignments may differ from past career paths.

Diversity

Belief Statement

Diversity should be valued and evident in our school district.

Guidelines for Decision Making

1. The district will acknowledge that each student is a unique individual and is entitled to an appropriate educational program.
2. The district will actively implement the Equal Opportunity Employment concept.
3. The district will respect individuality among staff.
4. The district will seek to maximize the strengths of diverse styles and strategies within a common district direction.
5. The district will expect each school/department to develop its own sense of community.
6. The district will encourage individuals to share their expertise outside the specific job descriptions.
7. The district will accord to all persons dignity, respect, and worth.

Recognition and Reward

Belief Statement

The accomplishments of employees should be valued and recognized in order to improve the quality of instruction and related services of our district.

Guidelines for Decision Making

1. The district will promote peer recognition of quality instruction and related services.
2. The district will implement a systematic, streamlined process for increasing awareness and pride in the many accomplishments of our district.
3. The district will utilize a representative group of all employees when designing a creative recognition program.
4. The district will recognize employees for excellence as a way to thank those employees and to encourage others to un-

lock or renew their potential for creativity, motivation, and involvement.

5. The district will create a climate where intrinsic rewards help employees feel a sense of accomplishment.
6. The district will make recognition public and timely and will monitor the success of the program.

APPENDIX B

A Vision for the School System in the Year 2000: Peel Board of Education, Ontario

Peel in the Year 2000

What kind of school system should Peel be in the coming decade? The question of Peel's future image was posed to staff in one of the central exercises of the strategic planning project. The responses mapped out a definite set of directions and provided a snapshot of Peel in the year 2000:

- The ideal Peel school system would be a leader in education, with a reputation as a dynamic, innovative, forward-thinking, and responsive organization. We would lead with flexibility, confidence, and skill in planning and problem solving.
- The school system would be humane, compassionate, supportive, and cohesive and would treat both clients and staff as responsible individuals.
- As a good employer, Peel would have realistic expectations, recognize excellence, and emphasize teamwork.
- We would reach out to all our communities and target groups by making the best use of good communications, public relations, and community resources. In addition, these communities would be supported by the school system's educational programs and services.

Source: "Directions for Renewal." Strategic planning by the Peel (Ontario) Board of Education. June 26, 1990, pp. 9–10.

151

- High-quality programs would focus on student-centered classrooms, "active" learning, and basic skills. The class of the year 2000 would be small and outfitted with new technology to aid the learning process.
- The board would be divided into smaller units, or decision making would be significantly decentralized, to focus more on the neighborhood school. Technology would connect the system and reduce paperwork and bureaucracy.
- Adequate funding would help end overcrowding, and resources would be focused on the schools to ensure their continuing success.

APPENDIX C

Our Values:
Center for Creative Leadership
Greensboro, North Carolina

Our Mission

The Center for Creative Leadership is a nonprofit educational institution founded in 1970 in Greensboro, North Carolina. Our mission is to encourage and develop creative leadership and effective management for the good of society overall.

We accomplish our mission through research, training, and publication, with emphasis on the widespread, innovative application of the behavioral sciences to the challenges facing the leaders of today and tomorrow.

Our Goals

* To contribute significantly to the theoretical and practical knowledge relevant to creative leadership.
* To improve the practice of leadership and the effectiveness of management across a broad range of organizations and groups, both public and private.
* To build a robust professional organization capable of achieving our institutional mandate over the long term, with particular regard for the development of individual staff members.

Source: Center for Creative Leadership, 1991. All rights reserved.

153

Our Values

Our Work Should Serve Society

We expect our work to make a difference in the quality of leadership in the world. To that end, we try to discover what is most important to do and focus our resources for the greatest, most enduring benefit. In doing this, we continually remind ourselves of the inherent worth of all people. We consider it our responsibility to be attentive to the unique needs of leaders who are women or members of minority groups.

To make a difference in the world and to turn ideas into action, we must be pioneers in our field, contributors of knowledge, creators of solutions, explorers of ideas, and risk takers [on] behalf of society.

Our Mission and Our Clients Deserve Our Best

We expect our service to our clients to be worthy, vigorous, resourceful, courteous, and reliable. In the pursuit of our mission, we intend to be a healthy, creative organization with the financial and inner resources needed to produce our best work.

We require ourselves to abide by the highest professional standards and to look beyond the letter of professional guidelines to their spirit. This includes being forthright and candid with every client and program participant, scrupulously guarding the confidentiality of sensitive personal and organizational information and truthfully representing our capabilities to prospective clients.

Our Organization Should Be a Good Place to Work

To demand the best of ourselves, and to attract, stimulate, and keep the best people, we believe we must make an environment that will support innovation, experimentation, and the taking of appropriate risks. As an organization, we should prize the creative participation of each member of our staff. We should welcome the open exchange of ideas and foster the practice of careful listening. We have a duty to actively encourage the personal well-being and the professional development of every person who works here. We should, therefore, maximize the authority and responsibility each person has to continue to make an ever-greater contribution. Our policies should be implemented sensitively and consistently.

We Should Do Our Work with Regard for One Another

We recognize the interdependence of everyone who works here, and we expect ourselves to treat one another with respect, candor, kindness, and a sense of the importance of teamwork. We should foster a spirit of service within the staff so that we may better serve the world at large.

APPENDIX D

Reflections on a Democratic Structure for Leadership in New Schools

How to start the process of imagining. . . a new school is no mystery, because what people need in a work organization is known: to be free, to be valued, to be challenged, to grow, to assume responsibility, to be secure, to be rewarded, to be in touch with their true selves. Such an organization is possible; it is within people's own power to create and implement if they choose to do so. We are convinced that it is necessary to move in the direction of organizations for people if excellence in performance and freedom for human beings are to be achieved.

Initially, we want to assert a small number of propositions that we feel are imperative in imagining a new school.

1. *A new school must be built on the assumption of the consent of the governed.* This concept is troublesome chiefly because it is strange. Yet if any organization should reflect democratic ideals, it is the school. Designated leaders, such as the principal, should be chosen by teachers. The professional staff of the school unit should choose their new colleagues. The professional staff is a work team of mature adults. They cannot manifest professional responsibility in an oligarchy.

Source: David L. Clark and Judith M. Meloy, "Renouncing Bureaucracy: A Democratic Structure for Leadership in Schools" in Thomas J. Sergiovanni and John H. Moore (eds.), *Schooling for Tomorrow: Directing Reforms to Issues that Count* (Boston: Allyn & Bacon, 1989). Reprinted with permission of the publisher.

2. A new school must be built on shared authority and responsibility, not delegation of authority and responsibility. The responsibility for a new school lies with the professional staff of the school, not solely or even predominantly with a designated leader. If the new school is a team enterprise, then the key actors on the team change from day to day and activity to activity. If there is to be delegation of authority, it must come from the team to the individual. If specialists in subject areas, or curriculum, or administration are to take on special spheres of responsibility, that assignment must be made by the staff of the school.

3. The staff of a new school must trade assignments and work in multiple groups to remain in touch with the school as a whole. The role of principal, head teacher, or chair should ordinarily be assumed for relatively short periods. The staff should include many individuals whose experience includes terms of work in administration and instructional development as well as classroom teaching. The work groups formed within the staff should provide opportunities to interact with a variety of colleagues on a variety of problems.

4. Formal rewards to the staff—salary, tenure, forms of promotion—should be under the control of the staff of the new school as a whole. There is no perfectly satisfactory way to distribute differential rewards, but no one is in a better position to deal with this difficult issue than a group of colleagues. Peer evaluation and decision making may end in the decision to reduce individual distinctions and emphasize group distinctions, **or** it may not. In either event, the power tools of formal rewards **and** recognition must not be controlled by an individual outside the group. The problem is a professional issue of self-determination.

5. The goals of the new school must be formulated and agreed to through group consensus. The professional staff is responsible for negotiating the acceptability of the goals to the school community. Although formal goals probably have little to do with organizational efficacy, the school needs to represent itself to its political constituency and clarify, for itself, its raison d'être. The school *is* the professional staff, acting both individually and collectively. The staff is responsible for negotiating the relationship of individual goals to the goals of the school as an organization, translating those into programs, and subsequently expressing the goals and programs to other responsible agents and agencies in an intelligible and acceptable form.

We are going to stop with this short list of "musts." They represent sufficiently the basic change in orientation that we feel is necessary to the "new school." If they were implemented, schools would be operating on the basis of:

- Democracy
- Group authority and accountability
- Variability, generality, and interactivity in work assignment
- Self-discipline and control exercised individually and collectively
- Group commitment to and consensus about organizational goals and means.

References

Albritton, M. *De Zavala Elementary School: A Committed Community.* Case study, Department of Education, Trinity University, 1991.

Barnard, C. *The Functions of the Executive.* Cambridge, Mass.: Harvard University Press, 1958. Originally published 1938.

Barth, R. *Improving Schools from Within.* San Francisco: Jossey-Bass, 1990.

Benjamin, M. *Splitting the Difference: Compromise and Integrity in Ethics and Politics.* Lawrence: University of Kansas Press, 1990.

Benne, K. D. "Democratic Ethics and Social Engineering." *Progressive Education,* 1949, *27* (7), 201–206.

Bennis, W. "Leadership Theory and Administrative Behavior: The Problem of Authority." *Administrative Science Quarterly,* 1959, *4* (2), 259–301.

Bennis, W. *Why Leaders Can't Lead: The Unconscious Conspiracy Continues.* San Francisco: Jossey-Bass, 1989.

Bennis, W., and Nanus, B. *Leaders: The Strategies for Taking Charge.* New York: HarperCollins, 1985.

Block, P. *The Empowered Manager.* San Francisco: Jossey-Bass, 1987.

Blumberg, A. *School Administration as Craft.* Needham Heights, Mass.: Allyn & Bacon, 1989.

Blumer, I. *School-Based Improvement Implications for Superintendents' Leadership.* Boston: Massachusetts Department of Education, 1989.

Boyer, E. (ed.). *Campus Life in Search of Community*. Princeton, N.J.: Carnegie Foundation for the Advancement of Teaching, 1990.

Brookover, W. B., and Lezotte, L. W. *Changes in School Characteristics Coincident with Changes in School Achievement*. Institute for Research on Teaching, Michigan State University, 1979.

Burns, J. M. *Leadership*. New York: HarperCollins, 1978.

Camenisch, P. F. "On Being a Professional, Morally Speaking." In A. Flores (ed.), *Professional Ideals*. Belmont, Calif.: Wadsworth, 1988.

Clark, D. L., and Meloy, J. M. "Renouncing Bureaucracy: A Democratic Structure for Leadership in Schools." In T. J. Sergiovanni and J. H. Moore (eds.), *Schooling for Tomorrow: Directing Reforms to Issues That Count*. Needham Heights, Mass.: Allyn & Bacon, 1989.

Csikszentmihalyi, M. *Flow: The Psychology of Optimal Experience*. New York: HarperCollins, 1990.

Darling-Hammond, L., and Sclam, E. "Policy and Supervision." In C. Glickman (ed.), *Supervision in Transition*. Alexandria, Va.: Association for Supervision and Curriculum Development, forthcoming.

Deal, T. E. "The Symbolism of Effective Schools." *Elementary School Journal*, 1985, *85* (5), 601–619.

Deal, T. E. "The Culture of Schools." In L. T. Scheive and M. B. Schoenheit (eds.), *Leadership: Examining the Elusive*. Alexandria, Va.: Association for Supervision and Curriculum Development, 1987.

Deal, T. E., and Peterson, K. D. *The Principal's Role in Shaping School Culture*. Washington, D.C.: U.S. Department of Education, 1990.

Deci, E. L., and Ryan, R. M. *Intrinsic Motivation and Self-Determination in Human Behavior*. New York: Plenum Press, 1985.

de Pree, M. *Leadership Is an Art*. New York: Doubleday, 1989.

Edmonds, R. R. "Effective Schools for the Urban Poor." *Educational Leadership*, 1979, *37* (2), 15–18, 20–24.

Etzioni, A. *Modern Organizations*. Englewood Cliffs, N.J.: Prentice-Hall, 1964.

Etzioni, A. *The Moral Dimension: Toward a New Economics.* New York: Free Press, 1988.

Flores, A. "What Kind of Person Should a Professional Be?" In A. Flores (ed.), *Professional Ideals.* Belmont, Calif.: Wadsworth, 1988.

Frankena, W. K. *Ethics.* Englewood Cliffs, N.J.: Prentice-Hall, 1973.

Gallup Organization. Survey conducted for the Princeton Religion Research Center, Princeton, N.J., March 11–20, 1988.

Garcia, A. Unpublished case study material, Department of Education, Trinity University, 1988.

Gilligan, C. *In a Different Voice.* Cambridge, Mass.: Harvard University Press, 1982.

Greenberg, S. "So You Want to Talk Theory?" Paper presented at the annual meeting of the American Educational Research Association, Boston, 1985.

Greene, D., and Lepper, M. "How to Turn Play into Work." *Psychology Today,* 1974, *8* (4), 49–52.

Greenfield, W. "The Micropolitics of Leadership in an Urban Elementary School." Paper presented at the annual meeting of the American Educational Research Association, Chicago, 1991.

Greenleaf, R. K. *Servant Leadership.* New York: Paulist Press, 1977.

Grimmitt, P. B., Rostad, O. P., and Ford, B. "Supervision: A Transformational Perspective," In C. Glickman (ed.), *Supervision in Transition.* Alexandria, Va.: Association for Supervision and Curriculum Development, forthcoming.

Guy, M. E. *Ethical Decision Making in Everyday Work Situations.* New York: Quorum Books, 1990.

Habermas, J. *Moral Consciousness and Communicative Action.* (Trans. C. Lenhardt and S. W. Nicholsen.) Cambridge, Mass.: MIT Press, 1990.

Hackman, J. R., and Oldham, G. "Motivation Through the Design of Work: A Test of a Theory." *Organizational Behavior and Human Performance,* 1976, *16* (2), 250–279.

Hackman, J. R., Oldham, G., Johnson, R., and Purdy, K. "A New Strategy for Job Enrichment." *California Management Review,* 1975, *17* (4), 57–71.

Haller, E. J., and Strike, K. A. *An Introduction to Educational Admin-istration: Social, Legal, and Ethical Perspectives.* White Plains, N.Y.: Longman, 1986.

Hampel, J. "The Administrator as Servant: A Model for Leadership Development." Unpublished manuscript, Department of Education, San Diego State University, 1988.

Hargreaves, A. "Contrived Collegiality and the Culture of Teaching." Paper presented at the annual meeting of the Canadian Society for the Study of Education, Quebec City, Quebec, 1989.

Hechinger, F. M. "About Education." *New York Times*, Nov. 7, 1990, p. B14.

Hersey, P., and Blanchard, K. H. *Management of Organizational Behavior: Utilizing Human Resources.* (5th ed.) Englewood Cliffs, N.J.: Prentice-Hall, 1988.

Herzberg, F. *Work and the Nature of Man.* New York: World, 1966.

Herzberg, F., Mausner, B., and Snyderman, B. *The Motivation to Work.* New York: Wiley, 1959.

Hesse, Herman. *The Journey to the East.* New York: Farrar, Straus & Giroux, 1956.

Hill, P. T., Foster, G. E., and Gendler, T. *High Schools with Character.* Santa Monica, Calif.: The RAND Corporation, 1990.

Hills, J. *The Preparation of Educational Leaders: What's Needed and What's Next.* Columbus, Ohio: University Council for Educational Administration, 1982.

Ihara, C. K. "Collegiality as a Professional Virtue." In A. Flores (ed.), *Professional Ideals.* Belmont, Calif.: Wadsworth, 1988.

Johnson, S. M. *Teachers at Work: Achieving Success in Our Schools.* New York: Basic Books, 1990.

Kant, I. *Foundations of the Metaphysics of Morals.* (Trans. L. W. Beck.) New York: Bobbs-Merrill, 1959. (Originally published 1785).

Kaufman, D. R., and Richardson, B. L. *Achievement and Women: Challenging the Assumptions.* New York: Free Press, 1982.

Kelly, R. E. "In Praise of Followers." *Harvard Business Review*, 1988, *88* (6), 142–148.

Kerr, S. "Substitutes for Leadership: Some Implications for Organizational Design." *Organizational and Administrative Sciences*, 1977, *8*, 135–146.

Lam, D. *Reinventing School Leadership — Humble Pie.* National Center for Educational Leadership, Harvard University, 1990.

Lewis, H. *A Question of Values.* New York: HarperCollins, 1990.

Lieberman, A. (ed.). *Building a Professional Culture in Schools.* Vol. 1. New York: Teachers College Press, 1988.

Lieberman, A., and Miller, L. *Teachers, Their World and Their Work.* Alexandria, Va.: Association for Supervision and Curriculum Development, 1984.

Lipsitz, J. *Successful Schools for Young Adolescents.* New Brunswick, N.J.: Transaction Press, 1984.

Little, J. W. "Teachers as Colleagues." In V. Richardson-Koehler (ed.), *Educator's Handbook: A Research Perspective.* White Plains, N.Y.: Longman, 1987.

Lockwood, A. T. "Central Park East Secondary School, NYC: Emphasis on Personalization." *Focus on Change*, 1990, *2* (3), p. 9.

Lortie, D. C. *Schoolteacher: A Sociological Study.* Chicago: University of Chicago Press, 1975.

Louv, R. "Hope in Hell's Classroom." *New York Times Magazine*, Nov. 25, 1990, pp. 30–33, 63–67, and 74–75.

MacIntyre, A. *After Virtue.* Notre Dame, Ind.: University of Notre Dame Press, 1981.

March, J. G. "How We Talk and How We Act: Administrative Theory and Administrative Life." In T. J. Sergiovanni and J. E. Corbally (eds.), *Leadership and Organizational Culture.* Urbana: University of Illinois Press, 1984.

Merton, R. *Social Theory and Social Structure.* New York: Free Press, 1968.

Miller, J. B. *Toward a New Psychology of Women.* Boston: Beacon Press, 1986.

Miller, L. M. *American Spirit: Visions of a New Corporate Culture.* New York: Morrow, 1984.

Mintzberg, H. *The Structure of Organizations.* New York: Wiley, 1979.

Mintzberg, H. "Crafting Strategy." *Harvard Business Review*, 1987, *87* (4), 66–75.

Mustain, G. "Botton-Drawer Bureau." *Washington Monthly*, Sept. 1990, p. 14.

Peters, T. "Engineers Must Stop Bureaucratic Urge." *San Antonio Light*, Aug. 1, 1990, p. 11B.

Peters, T. J., and Waterman, R. H., Jr. *In Search of Excellence: Lessons from America's Best-Run Companies.* New York: HarperCollins, 1982.

Pondy, L. R. "Leadership Is a Language Game." In M. W. McCall, Jr., and M. M. Lombardo (eds.), *Leadership: Where Else Can We Go?* Durham, N.C.: Duke University Press, 1978.

Rawls, J. *A Theory of Justice.* Cambridge, Mass.: Harvard University Press, 1971.

Reddin, W. J. *Managerial Effectiveness.* New York: McGraw-Hill, 1970.

Rosenholtz, S. J. *Teachers' Workplace: The Social Organization of Schools.* White Plains, N.Y.: Longman, 1989.

Ruggiero, V. R. *The Art of Thinking.* (2nd ed.) New York: Harper-Collins, 1988.

Sarason, S. "Forging the Classroom's 'Constitution.'" *Education Week*, Oct. 24, 1990, p. 36.

Sashkin, M. *Strategies for School Improvement.* Washington, D.C.: U.S. Department of Education, 1990.

Schein, E. H. *Organizational Culture and Leadership.* San Francisco: Jossey-Bass, 1985.

Schön, D. A. "Leadership as Reflection in Action." In T. J. Sergiovanni and J. E. Corbally (eds.), *Leadership and Organizational Culture.* Urbana: University of Illinois Press, 1984.

Selznick, P. *Leadership in Administration.* Berkeley: University of California Press, 1957.

Senge, P. M. *The Fifth Dimension: The Art and Practice of the Learning Organization.* New York: Doubleday, 1990a.

Senge, P. M. "The Leader's New Work: Building a Learning Organization." *Sloan Management Review*, 1990b, *32* (1), 7–23.

Sergiovanni, T. J. "Factors Which Affect Satisfaction and Dissatisfaction of Teachers." *Journal of Educational Administration*, 1967, *5* (1), 66–87.

Sergiovanni, T. J. "Leadership and Excellence in Schooling." *Educational Leadership*, 1984, *41* (5), 4–14.

Sergiovanni, T. J. "Will We Ever Have a TRUE Profession?" *Educational Leadership*, 1987, *44* (8), 44–51.

Sergiovanni, T. J. "Science and Scientism in Supervision and Teaching." *Journal of Curriculum and Supervision,* 1989, *4* (2), 43–105.

Sergiovanni, T. J. *Value-Added Leadership: How to Get Extraordinary Performance in Schools.* Orlando, Fla.: Harcourt Brace Jovanovich, 1990.

Shakeshaft, C. *Women in Educational Administration.* Newbury Park, Calif.: Sage, 1987.

Shils, E. A. "Centre and Periphery." In *The Logic of Personal Knowledge: Essays Presented to Michael Polanyi.* New York: Routledge & Kegan Paul, 1961.

Starratt, R. J. *The Drama of Schooling, the Schooling of Drama.* New York: Falmer Press, 1990.

Stogdill, R. M. *Handbook of Leadership.* New York: Free Press, 1974.

Telegram and Gazette (Worcester, Mass.) Dec. 6, 1990, p. 6.

Tom, A. R. *Teaching as a Moral Craft.* White Plains, N.Y.: Longman, 1984.

Tyack, D., and Hansot, E. *Managers of Virtue: Public Leadership in America, 1820–1980.* New York: Basic Books, 1982.

Vaill, P. "The Purposing of High-Performance Systems." In T. J. Sergiovanni and J. E. Corbally (eds.), *Leadership and Organizational Culture.* Urbana: University of Illinois Press, 1984.

Van de Kamp Nohl, M. "Miracle on 4th Street." *Milwaukee Magazine,* 1989, *14,* 72–82.

Veblen, T. *The Theory of the Leisure Class.* Boston: Houghton Mifflin, 1973.

Weick, K. E. "The Concept of Loose Coupling: An Assessment." *Organizational Theory Dialogue,* Dec. 1986, 8–12.

Weick, K. E., and McDaniel, R. R., Jr. "How Professional Organizations Work: Implications for School Organization and Management." In T. J. Sergiovanni and J. H. Moore (eds.), *Schooling for Tomorrow: Directing Reforms to Issues That Count.* Needham Heights, Mass.: Allyn & Bacon, 1989.

Yatvin, J. "Let Teachers 'Re-invent the Wheel.'" *Education Week,* Sept. 19, 1990, p. 25.

Zaleznik, A. *The Managerial Mystique: Restoring Leadership in Business.* New York: HarperCollins, 1989.

Index

167

P

Peel Board of Education (Ontario), 111, 151
Peters, T. J., 5, 93
Peterson, K., 75
Phi Delta Kappa, 102
Piersall, C., 17, 18
Pondy, L., 140
Principle of beneficience, 105
Principle of justice, 165
Professional ideal, 52–56; administrators and, 55; as virtue, 55
Professionalism: dimensions of, 90–92; as source of authority, 35–40; standards for, 41–42; as virtue, 52–56

R

RAND Corporation, 99
Rawls, J., 106, 107, 108, 111, 117
Richardson, B. L., 135
Robert E. Lee High School (San Antonio), 138
Rodriguez, M. H., 116, 128
Rosenfeld, H., 114
Rosenholtz, S. J., 86, 88
Riggiero, V. R., 109, 110, 111
Ryan, R., 24

S

San Antonio School (Dade City), 17
San Juan Day School (San Juan Pueblo), 130
Schein, E. H., 46
Scholastic Aptitude Test (SAT), 100
Schon, D., 14
School: as community, 45–48, 118, 125; covenants in, 73, 102; culture, 88–90, 99; effective, 99; focus, 99–102; as instructional delivery systems, 45, 46; managerial imperative, 104–105; moral imperative, 104–105; virtuous, 99, 112–118; zoned, 100–101

School culture, 88–90
Schwarz, P., 113
Second categorical imperative, 106
Selznick, P., 43, 72
Senge, P. M., xii, xiii
Servant leadership, 116, 117, 122, 125, 136; defined, 124–125; examples of, 116, 120–123, 128, 138; misperceptions of, 126; and moral authority, 138; principles of, 129–135
Shakeshaft, C., 136
Shoreham-Wading River Central School District, 40, 42
Snyderman, B., 59
Soderberg, L., 5
Starratt, R. J., 47
Stewardship, 120–139; in practice, 120–123, 138
Stogdill, R., 2
Strike, K., 33, 34

T

Taft Elementary School (Joliet), 132
Townsend, R., 10, 11
Trained incapacity, 4–5

U

Utilitarianism, 19, 20

V

Vaill, P., 73, 129
Values, 9, 11–13; official, 13; professional, 52–56; sacred, 12, 15; secular, 12, 14; semiofficial, 13; unofficial, 13
Value-Added Leadership, 69
Van de Kamp Nohl, M., 48
Veil of ignorance, 106
Virtuous school, 99; characteristics of, 112–118; moral principles, 104–110
Vista Unified School District, California, 10

W

Waterman, R. H., 93
Weick, K., 52, 93
Wells High School (Wells), 44
West Warwich High School (West
    Warwich), 84
Work Itself as Substitute for
    Leadership Inventory, 65–66

Y

Yatvin, J., 115, 118

Z

Zaleznik, A., 3, 4